the low brass player's guide to DOUBLING

Micah Everett

Foreword: Les Benedict

Contributing Authors:

Frank Gazda

Alexander Lapins

Marc Dickman

Jeffrey Cortazzo

Brian French

J. Mark Thompson

The Low Brass Player's Guide to Doubling
Micah Everett

MPM 18-020
$34.95
© 2014 Mountain Peak Music

2700 Woodlands Village Blvd. #300-124
Flagstaff, Arizona 86001
www.mountainpeakmusic.com

This publication is protected by Copyright Law.
Do not photocopy, scan or share PDFs. All rights reserved.

ISBN 978-1-935510-72-7

Table of Contents

Foreword i

Acknowledgments ii

Introduction 1

Chapter 1: General Considerations 5

Chapter 2: Tenor Trombonists Doubling on Bass Trombone 13

Chapter 3: Bass Trombonists Doubling on Tenor Trombone 26

Chapter 4: Doubling on Two or More Sizes of the Same Instrument 33

Chapter 5: Trombonists Doubling on Euphonium 35

Chapter 6: Trombonists Doubling on Tuba (Frank Gazda) 52

Chapter 7: Tuba Players Doubling on Euphonium (Alexander Lapins) 68

Chapter 8: Euphonium and Tuba Players Doubling on Trombone (Marc Dickman) ... 73

Chapter 9: Alto Trombone 88

Chapter 10: Contrabass Trombone (Jeffrey Cortazzo) 97

Chapter 11: Bass Trumpet (Brian French) 105

Chapter 12: Cimbasso (J. Mark Thompson) 115

Appendix A: Daily Practice Regimens 125

Appendix B: Sample Scale Routines 128

Appendix C: Bass Trombone Resources
    Targeted Fundamentals 135
    Fingering Charts 141
    Overtone Series Charts 145

Appendix D: Tenor Trombone Resources
    Targeted Fundamentals 147
    Fingering Chart 150

Overtone Series Chart..152

Appendix E: Euphonium and Baritone Horn Resources
Targeted Fundamentals..153
Fingering Chart...156
Overtone Series Chart..158

Appendix F: Tuba and Cimbasso Resources
Targeted Fundamentals..159
Fingering Charts...171
Overtone Series Charts...179

Appendix G: Alto Trombone Resources
Targeted Fundamentals..183
Fingering Chart...186
Overtone Series Chart..188

Appendix H: Contrabass Trombone Resources
Targeted Fundamentals..189
Fingering Charts...195
Overtone Series Charts...199

Appendix I: Bass Trumpet Resources
Targeted Fundamentals..201
Fingering Charts...207
Overtone Series Charts...211

About the Authors..213

Foreword

This much needed book fills a gap for low brass players in what has become a necessity for teachers and performers alike. At one time, doubling on brass instruments was a rarity, but in today's world it is common to be passed over if one doesn't play at least one double, and usually more than one. Micah Everett and company tackle this issue in an organized, comprehensive, and systematic manner. Each section gives the would-be doubler a great head start over the traditional trial and error techniques of the past, and the challenges presented by each instrument are thoroughly explained. From motivation for doubling, to types and quality of instruments, to suggested materials and practice techniques, this book is a winner.

Les Benedict

Low Brass Artist

The Low Brass Player's Guide to Doubling

Acknowledgements

A project of this magnitude is never a solo endeavor, so I must express appreciation to the many individuals who made this book possible, including David Vining of Mountain Peak Music, who contacted me after reading some of my blog posts on doubling and asked if I would like to expand those ideas into a book-length project. One of my main reasons for blogging was to develop my "writing chops" and hopefully one day produce something longer, more substantial, and in print. I am grateful for the opportunity to do just that, and on a topic that has very much defined my career as a low brass player.

I owe much to Dr. Edward R. Bahr, Professor of Low Brass (retired) at Delta State University. Not only was his teaching formative for my low brass playing, but his many connections in our professional community were vital in the early stages of my career. Most importantly for the present subject, "Doc" was singularly responsible for encouraging (actually, more like *demanding*) that I take up euphonium doubling in a serious way after hearing my unpracticed dabbling on the instrument (of the kind that I warn against in this book). That decision truly set the course for the remainder of my career, and I am thankful for Dr. Bahr's encouragement and friendship, then and now.

My two applied teachers in graduate school at the University of North Carolina at Greensboro (UNCG) further developed my abilities not only in brass playing and teaching generally, but particularly as a doubler. Dr. Randy Kohlenberg supervised my initial performing work as an alto trombonist and encouraged me to take up bass trombone. He was reluctantly supportive of my euphonium doubling, realizing its importance for my career but also lamenting the negative effects it sometimes had on my trombone playing. He helped me recognize and negotiate certain key differences in approach between the cylindrical and conical low brasses, concepts which now permeate my playing and teaching and which appear throughout this book. Dr. Dennis AsKew was willing to take me on as a euphonium student even though that was not my primary instrument at the graduate level. His teaching helped me to further understand and master differences between the trombone and euphonium, particularly with regard to articulation, while an independent study he supervised on euphonium and tuba pedagogy and literature prepared me for life and work teaching all of the low brass instruments. The instruction and support provided by all three of these men have been invaluable, and although they were not directly consulted during the preparation of this book,

The Low Brass Player's Guide to Doubling

their teaching can be found throughout its pages.

My colleagues at the University of Mississippi have kindly offered encouragement, and I am particularly grateful to our late department chair, Dr. Charles R. Gates, who from our very first meeting both encouraged and admonished me to do big things. I certainly hope this project qualifies. To my students both current and former—at Ole Miss, the University of Louisiana at Monroe, the University of Northern Iowa, Elon University, and at UNCG—you have provided the primary forum in which I have developed the ideas presented here. I often feel I have learned as much from you as you have from me.

Although the majority of this text is my own, six coauthors contributed individual chapters. Jeff Cortazzo, Dr. Marc Dickman, Brian French, Dr. Frank Gazda, Dr. Alexander Lapins, and Dr. J. Mark Thompson are all experienced players, teachers, and doublers, and each has expertise in areas where I am lacking. This is a better book because of their contributions, and I appreciate their willingness to participate in its creation.

Finally, to my wife Jennifer and my son Brody, who have patiently endured my absence (even when working at home!) while I worked so long on this and other writing and performing endeavors, I am always thankful for your love, encouragement, patience, and prayers. I am a better man because you are in my life. Even though I sometimes find it difficult to wear all the different hats of musician, teacher, husband, father, and churchman (not necessarily in that—or always the same—order), I thank God for the opportunity to even try to do it all.

Oxford, Mississippi

August 2014

Introduction

Before taking up a secondary instrument, strive to cultivate solid fundamental brass playing on your primary instrument. This basic proficiency on your primary instrument is a prerequisite for successful doubling. Once that foundation is established, you might decide to branch out into playing one or more secondary instruments. Here are a number of good reasons to play multiple low brass instruments, beginning with the higher objectives related to personal enrichment and proceeding to those which appeal to our baser motives (such as making more money).

Personal Enjoyment

Personal enjoyment is a foundational motivation for making music and should be a primary factor in choosing to double. While doubling provides opportunities for developing musicianship, the initial learning process will no doubt include some drudgery as you cultivate fundamental playing skills on the new instrument. If you can learn to enjoy the process, learning to double will be more pleasant. More importantly, maintaining a sense of joy throughout your career is vital to your long-term happiness in the music business, regardless of the number of instruments you play.

Broader Musicianship

To some, the idea of specializing on a single instrument sounds like a life with limited musical horizons. Each low brass instrument has interesting players, teachers, and literature to its credit, and the breadth of musical ideas possible on each instrument increases with each passing day. Multiply that breadth by two, three, four or more instruments, and the performers, pedagogical ideas, repertoire, and skills that enter your orbit increases dramatically. By performing well on several instruments, doublers become more complete musicians, regardless of the instrument being played at any given moment.

Exposure to New Literature

A key benefit of doubling for low brass players is exposure to new literature, both for instruction and performance. Low brass instruments naturally have a large body of shared repertoire, but each instrument also has solo, chamber works, and study materials which might be unfamiliar to players of the other instruments. Taking up a secondary instrument will introduce you to new composers,

The Low Brass Player's Guide to Doubling

repertoire, and ideas that will enhance your musicianship.

One of the most obvious literature-related benefits of doubling comes in the programming of solo and chamber performances. When you learn a secondary instrument well enough to perform on that instrument as a recitalist, the number of quality works available to you doubles! Instead of returning repeatedly to old standbys, the skilled doubler can give performances of interesting and challenging solo literature and go for years without repeating a piece. Likewise, while the brass quintet is a versatile ensemble, its available repertoire is increased when the trombonist can double on euphonium, or the player on the bottom part can play both tuba and bass trombone, or even cimbasso. Smaller groups such as brass trios benefit greatly when players can choose between multiple instruments; the usual trumpet/horn/tenor trombone group can quickly adopt a darker and warmer sound by changing to a flugelhorn/horn/bass trombone instrumentation. Even like-instrument ensembles such as trombone quartets and tuba quartets can add variety by using doubling instruments. Each of these instrumentation changes brings new choices of timbres and literature.

Additional Performance Opportunities

Doubling makes new performing opportunities available to you in two ways: by enabling you to work in different types of ensembles, and by allowing you to assume different roles in settings with which you are already familiar. Perhaps the most common example of doubling in different types of ensembles is the tuba or euphonium player who takes up trombone to perform in jazz and popular groups. Trombone players should consider that pit orchestras, studio work, and sometimes even big bands require a single player to double on bass trombone and tuba or tenor and bass trombones, and sometimes more than two instruments. Playing more instruments makes different types of chamber ensembles available to you, and as mentioned previously, can even allow players to vary the instrumentation of existing groups for interesting tonal effects and greater marketability.

Sometimes taking up a secondary instrument allows you to occupy different or modified roles in familiar settings. For example, suppose a tenor trombonist moves to a new city in which there are more competent tenor trombonists than available work, but a relatively small number of working bass trombonists. Adding a bass trombone double might lead to more gigs more quickly than continuing to play tenor trombone only. Doubling on alto trombone is a necessity for those wanting to play first trombone in symphony orchestras, and the cimbasso is an increasingly expected double for tubists. In concert bands and brass bands, the trombones and conical low brasses occupy very

2

The Low Brass Player's Guide to Doubling

different places in the ensemble's tonal palette. Being able to play several instruments well enables you to experience all of these.

Improved Teaching Opportunities

The professional musician that works exclusively as a performer is exceedingly rare. Usually, the working musician must assemble a living from multiple income streams that will almost certainly include teaching. Musicians who develop competency on a secondary instrument are more competitive as they enter the job market. For example, a low brass player seeking employment as a school band director will be more likely to be hired and to succeed as a program's "brass person" if she is proficient on at least one instrument from the trombone and tuba families. Proficient performers might be employed as applied teachers at smaller colleges and universities on an adjunct basis, and a player who doubles on two or more low brass instruments will be a stronger candidate for such a position. A band or orchestra director with aspirations of conducting a collegiate ensemble will find that entry-level college positions often include applied teaching as part of the course load; a conductor who is an able and experienced performer will be a much stronger candidate for such positions and a doubler's application will be further enhanced. Given the fierce competition for academic jobs, the more hats one can wear, the better.

Cultivating multiple areas of teaching competency is vital even for those who pursue careers as college and university professors. With full-time, tenure-track positions becoming increasingly rare, many music departments will hire a professor of low brass rather than specialists on both trombone and tuba, much less euphonium. Players with demonstrated ability and experience on two or more low brass instruments will be stronger candidates for such positions.

For the full-time performer who teaches private lessons, the importance of doubling is more obvious and more directly remunerative. If you can play multiple instruments you can accept students on all of those instruments. Some schools hire private teachers to teach on site, even during the school day, and a competent teacher of several instruments might be preferred to a specialist on only one.

Improved Teaching Abilities

Doubling requires that you have a secure understanding of the fundamental aspects of playing, including the air, embouchure formation, articulation, etc. Successful performing on multiple instruments requires a more thoughtful approach to these basic elements, making you better able to recognize, diagnose, and correct weaknesses in your students' playing. Similarly, doubling gives you a more informed understanding of the problems experienced by young students. Taking up a secondary instrument allows you to experience some of these challenges again with the ears and experience of a more seasoned musician. The process of working out problems and developing proficiency on a doubling instrument provides excellent preparation for helping students solve similar problems.

As a doubler, you will be influenced by a larger variety of great performers and teachers, drawing from a broader pool of ideas to diagnose and correct problems in your own and your students' playing. The exposure to additional literature allows you to assign study materials and performance repertoire that will best address each student's needs. Doubling will also cause you to take a more thoughtful approach to both playing and teaching. The doubler must be aware at all times of the particular traps that might be encountered with the instrument being played at a given moment. Thus, doubling necessitates more thoughtful playing and leads to more thoughtful teaching, as you become more consciously aware of the peculiarities of each instrument and even begin to anticipate students' difficulties. Your resulting instruction becomes more effective on every instrument you teach.

More Money

Playing more instruments will increase your earning potential. I list this reason for doubling last not because it is unimportant or unworthy, but because the potential for greater income through doubling is usually the last objective to be realized. This benefit usually comes only after a period of individual practice, perhaps private study on the new instrument, and often, performances in amateur or student performing groups to "work the bugs out." Still, the earning potential is there, and given conditions in the present job market there often is no other choice but to double if a sufficient income is to be earned as a musician. Choose a secondary instrument that you like and that is in demand where you live, purchase the best instrument you can afford, devote time and effort to study and practice, and then enjoy the increased number of performing and teaching opportunities. In this book we will explore ways to help you do just that.

Chapter 1: General Considerations

In this chapter, we will consider ideas for crafting an overall approach to playing which will apply to all of your instruments, and develop a practice regimen that promotes optimum skill development on each instrument without exceeding your available time. Throughout this discussion I will favor broad concepts which can be tailored to meet your particular needs and objectives over details that will be covered in future chapters.

Organizing Principle: Designate One Primary Instrument

Playing multiple low brass instruments can be fun, exciting, and lucrative, but there are dangers lurking which can present themselves if you allow the diverse requirements of several instruments to bring about a loss of focus in your playing. When conceiving and structuring your practicing and playing, identify one instrument as your primary instrument with secondary instruments treated as departures from that one. All the low brass instruments share certain similarities, and doubling is easiest and most efficiently practiced when these similarities are identified. By using this approach, your primary instrument will receive the most comprehensive attention, with secondary instrument practice focused upon those areas where the instruments differ from one another. As you become more proficient at playing multiple instruments, resist the temptation to depart from this structure. Once you feel equally comfortable on two or more instruments, it can be tempting to abandon the concept of a primary instrument and consider *all* of your instruments are in some way primary. Players yielding to this enticement establish a rotation in which different instruments occupy the primary place on different days, or perhaps one in which every instrument is placed on equal footing, placing the daily fundamentals routine in flux. The stability promoted by the distinction between primary and secondary instruments is thus abandoned in favor of a routine and concept which is unstable. Having attempted a number of years ago to practice in this way, I found it to be completely unsatisfactory: the attempt to have five primary instruments yielded a result that was more like having five secondary instruments and *no* primary instrument. While I was able to eliminate a small amount of daily practice time spent on playing fundamentals, this advantage was offset by additional time spent addressing fundamental issues which presented themselves in other practice and performance materials—problems which did not normally arise with my former approach. I had become, in effect, a "jack of all trades and master of none."

Rightly dissatisfied with the result of my experiment, I resumed my earlier pattern of having one primary instrument and treating the others as a departure from that instrument. I have named this approach "jack of all trades and master of *one,*" because grounding your overall approach to brass playing in the requirements of a single instrument provides stability to your playing. Other instruments are introduced as modifications to that approach, but never as entirely separate entities. The result is a means of maintaining skills on multiple low brass instruments that is both efficient and effective, and which, when done well, leaves the listener unable to tell which of the instruments is the primary instrument.

Using this approach does not mean the primary instrument must always be the first one played each day. The instrument that is first in *priority* does not have to be first in *sequence.* Sometimes you will not have time to complete a thorough daily routine on your primary instrument before engaging in secondary instrument work, particularly when you have an early morning gig or lesson on a secondary instrument. In these situations, you might elect to perform a brief warm-up on the secondary instrument prior to the engagement, and then complete a more extended daily routine on your primary instrument later in the day. I am differentiating between a "warm-up" and a "daily routine" as follows: a warm-up can be quite brief and is performed on whatever instrument is needed for the day's first engagement in order to prepare the mind and body to play with focus and without injury; a daily routine is more extended, should focus upon the primary instrument, and is the forum for establishing and reinforcing your basic brass playing skills.

While an effective approach to doubling is focused upon a single primary instrument, there is no reason this must always be the same instrument for your entire career. Over time you might find yourself more frequently employed playing one of your secondary instruments. In such a situation, you might seriously consider a shift in focus, with the former secondary instrument moving into the primary role and the former primary instrument assuming a lesser place. While such a change might seem frightening, it is relatively painless. I usually maintain the large-bore tenor trombone as my primary instrument because it occupies the middle position among the five instruments I play. There have been times, however, when I was doing most of my performing on the bass trombone and moved that instrument into the primary role. During these periods I experienced a modest improvement in my bass trombone playing which served me well. While later circumstances dictated that I move the large-bore tenor trombone back into the primary place, much of the benefit to my bass trombone playing has been retained. This demonstrated to me that while centering one's playing upon a single primary instrument is the most effective approach to doubling, the identity of that primary instrument need not be fixed. It can be changed—and changed back—as needed, without lasting detrimental effects upon one's playing. Indeed, some long-term benefits might be realized.

Structuring Daily Practice

Effective doubling requires an approach to daily practice which is organized according to the primary/secondary instrument distinction just described. The core of this approach is extensive fundamentals practice with a thorough daily routine performed on the primary instrument, targeted work on fundamentals on secondary instruments, and scale and arpeggio practice on all instruments. These skills are then applied and further developed through practice of repertoire on both primary and secondary instruments (see the appendices for detailed descriptions and examples of each of these areas, organized by instrument).

The Primary Instrument Daily Routine

The core of the doubler's daily practice should be a comprehensive routine performed on the primary instrument addressing all of the basic physical and technical aspects of playing. While this routine includes some of the same activities as a warm-up, it is much broader than that, establishing all of the fundamental elements of brass playing in a way that can then be applied to further playing demands on the primary instrument and, by extension and modification, to secondary instruments. An effective daily routine generally requires twenty to sixty minutes to complete and need not be the first material played each day.

Targeted Fundamentals on Secondary Instruments

Targeted Fundamentals for secondary instruments should require no longer than seven to fifteen minutes and should be designed so that the characteristic sound of each instrument is achieved and reinforced, followed by exercises addressing differences between the primary and secondary instruments. Transferring shared techniques from one instrument to another is efficient and leaves sufficient time and chops for the remainder of the day's playing requirements.

Scales and Arpeggios

Practicing scales and arpeggios on every instrument you play should be part of your daily fundamentals work. While the notes of a given scale or arpeggio are the same on every instrument, each instrument has its own fingering patterns and peculiarities. Practicing scales and arpeggios on every instrument you play is the only way to ensure that these patterns are always executed with maximum accuracy.

Determining how to practice scales and arpeggios can be difficult, especially for the advanced player doubling on several instruments. I have committed well over two hundred different scales to memory and about half as many arpeggios, yet there is not enough time to practice each of these patterns daily on every instrument. Here are some suggestions for organizing scale and arpeggio practice:

1. Develop scale and arpeggio routines in each key area, which review all of the scales and arpeggios you know (or want to know) and practice one such routine daily. This ensures a review of every known scale and arpeggio every twelve days, providing ample practice of these necessary patterns with a minimal daily time commitment. I recommend organizing these routines by key area rather than by type of pattern (for example, practicing every major scale one day, every natural minor scale the next day, etc.), as the latter method of organization deprives the player of the ear training benefit of hearing the unique intervallic relationships in each scale and arpeggio each day. After all, being able to *hear* these patterns accurately is a prerequisite to being able to *execute* them accurately.

2. For the doubler, developing a rotation *within* the scale and arpeggio routines is a way to realize the benefits of scale and arpeggio practice on each instrument while limiting the necessary time commitment. For example, divide your scale routine into six sections, further dividing those sections between three instruments, playing two sections on each. As long as a given instrument is not used to play the same patterns during each practice session, over time you will master every pattern on every instrument while making the most efficient use of available practice time. Alternatively, you might choose to perform your entire scale and arpeggio routine on a different instrument each day. I have used a mix of these means of rotation, and find myself readily able to execute any desired pattern on each of my instruments. More importantly, I can immediately recognize and execute these

patterns in the context of real music. That is, after all, the main purpose of scale and arpeggio practice.

Between daily fundamentals work on primary and secondary instruments and regular practice of scales and arpeggios, you can easily find yourself spending thirty to fifty percent of your practice time on fundamentals. Occasionally that percentage can move even higher. While you might think this way of practicing leaves too little time for work on repertoire, I have found that spending a large amount of time reinforcing and extending basic playing skills greatly reduces the amount of time needed to master new music. Devoting a large percentage of your practice time to fundamentals is thus an extremely efficient way to practice, especially when managing the requirements of multiple instruments.

Repertoire Practice

Although a substantial length of time must be devoted to fundamental exercises each day, these are but a tool to facilitate great musicianship. Being able to execute extremes of range, flexibility, articulation, and speed in repetitive exercises is useless if you cannot deliver a comparable performance of music requiring the same skills. Repertoire thus demonstrates the limits of fundamental exercises, encouraging you to apply your capabilities in interesting and unexpected ways in order to achieve a desired musical result. Occasionally the challenges encountered in a certain piece will even reveal an area in which your daily routines are deficient and need to be adjusted—a fact you will want to discover in the practice room, not on the gig.

Repertoire must be practiced regularly and *on every instrument you play*. Regular fundamentals practice on every instrument combined with practice of repertoire on only some of the instruments is not sufficient. Practicing this way would make you a musician on some instruments and merely a technician on others; your musicianship would be truncated on those instruments where beautiful phrasing was not pursued first in the practice room.

Choose repertoire you enjoy and might like to perform. While there are times when a piece of music should be practiced because of a particular challenge it presents, or because it is on an audition list, or simply because it is a standard work that you simply ought to know, it is still easiest to practice playing a piece with great musicianship because you like it. Remember also that you are choosing music primarily for the practice room and not the concert hall, although you might want to think with more than one purpose in mind. Indeed, I find it quite helpful to keep music for at least one or two recital programs in my regular practice rotation. While these programs remain in an embryonic stage until a recital is actually scheduled, having a folder full of solo works on the stand, any of which might be used for a future performance, motivates me to begin developing both technical skills and musical ideas for these works, and to address areas of my technique which require improvement. You might choose to practice a regular rotation of favorite orchestral excerpts, jazz standards, or other materials that might be required on short notice for an audition or performance.

Choose music which forces you to address technical challenges, and particularly those where musical and technical challenges present themselves simultaneously. All brass players have areas of their playing which are weaker than others and which cause difficulty with both technical execution and the realization of musical objectives. While such weaknesses can sometimes be masked in performance, in the practice room they are best faced directly, through a combination of fundamental exercises to improve execution and repertoire which applies those same skills. In this case, method books, solo literature, excerpts, chamber music—anything which forces you to address the problem at hand in a musical fashion—can be used.

Choose music that corrects imbalances in your performing schedule. Having music for every instrument in the rotation can allow you to arrange your practice time to compensate for a performance schedule that is heavily tilted toward one instrument. The doubler on two instruments who is performing on one instrument every night and the other just once a month might devote the majority of repertoire practice to the second instrument, even while fundamentals practice remains essentially unchanged. Should the performance schedule become more balanced in the future, the practice regimen can be adjusted accordingly. For further recommendations for organizing both fundamentals and repertoire practice on multiple instruments, please consult Appendix A.

Tonal Range

An additional organizing principle to low brass doubling is the idea that all of these instruments have—or can have—the same basic tonal range. Of course, I do not mean to say that the lowest tuba notes sound good on the alto trombone (they are mostly false tones, after all) or that the highest alto trombone notes sound good on the tuba (they are usually mere squeaks). However, the player's buzz creates the note, and if you can buzz a pitch on one instrument you should be able to at least buzz it on another, even though the tone might be compromised. Strive to cultivate your tonal range in a

The Low Brass Player's Guide to Doubling

way that transcends the strengths and limitations of the instrument you are playing at a given moment. This approach makes moving from one instrument to the other much easier because you will not depend upon the instrument to produce a pitch, but only to provide the best, most responsive, and most characteristic sound when buzzing that pitch.

A Brief Word about Equipment

You will notice that I have mostly avoided making specific suggestions with regard to equipment (such as brands), preferring to make such recommendations in broad terms only. Every brass player strives to find the instrument, mouthpiece, and accessories that will facilitate playing with the greatest possible skill, efficiency, and freedom. This is true both for the specialist on a single instrument and for the doubler, though for the latter, realizing this goal becomes more complicated. The doubler must not only seek instruments that work well when considered individually but must also consider how well these instruments work together. A tenor trombonist, for example, might find an alto trombone that readily yields the desired sound and response, yet has certain characteristics (such as slide positions that are in wildly different places relative to the bell compared to the tenor trombone) that lead to a difficult transition between instruments. In such a scenario, the player might choose a different alto trombone that, while slightly inferior to the first in certain respects, does not feel as foreign compared to the tenor trombone. Similar conflicts can present themselves with nearly every primary/secondary instrument combination.

Price must also be considered. Not everyone can afford top of the line models for every instrument they play; a doubler can easily spend a year's salary (or more) to purchase an ideal wish list of instruments. Instead, consider secondhand instruments or instruments of slightly inferior brands in order to acquire a functional set of instruments that delivers satisfactory sounds in all situations.

Physiological differences between players and differences in playing situations must also be considered when choosing equipment. An instrument that enables one player to produce a great sound can yield an unsatisfactory sound for another, and an instrument that works in an orchestra might be inappropriate for a jazz band. The myriad options of alloys, valve designs, bore and bell sizes, etc., demonstrate that everybody's different, to say nothing of individual needs regarding mouthpieces.

Finally, brass instrument technology is constantly changing and developing. New instruments, mouthpieces, and design options are introduced regularly. New manufacturing firms are emerging with interesting innovations and, sadly, firms both old and new sometimes succumb to the difficult economic realities of the musical instrument market. Given the rapidity of development in the musical instrument industry, specific instrument recommendations can cause a book to become dated rather quickly, and given the different physiologies and playing situations of each player, they are often unhelpful. My aim instead is to make this book useful to as many people as possible for many years to come.

The Low Brass Player's Guide to Doubling

Chapter 2: Tenor Trombonists Doubling on Bass Trombone

At one time the question of "tenor or bass?" was an either/or question, with players choosing one or the other and rarely attempting both (the West Coast studio scene with its long tradition of multi-instrument doubling being a notable exception). With gigs becoming scarcer and more engagements specifically calling for a tenor/bass double, being able to play both tenor and bass trombones has become increasingly necessary. In this chapter and the one following, I will address this combination from both directions: the tenor trombonist doubling on bass, and the bass trombonist doubling on tenor.

A Suggestion Before Beginning: Low Range Development

The bass trombone will not automatically enable you to produce low notes that you cannot already play. The tenor and bass trombones share the same basic tonal range with different areas of emphasis, and it is the *player's buzz* which creates the pitch, not the instrument. If you can buzz a certain low note on the tenor trombone, you should be able to do so more easily on the bass trombone. If you cannot buzz that note on the tenor trombone, the bass trombone will probably not correct this problem for you.

If you want to take up bass trombone, begin by developing your low register on the tenor to the fullest possible extent. This way the bass trombone will serve as a more efficient and responsive amplifier for the vibrations you can already create, rather than being expected to magically generate a new skill. If the range requirements are largely mastered before you begin, development of the other skills necessary for bass trombone doubling will be relatively quick and easy.

Basic Similarities and Differences

As I have already noted, developing an accurate understanding of the similarities and differences between the instruments is vital, as efficient doubling requires that areas of similarity transfer from one instrument to the other, while differences are addressed with greater focus. The tenor and bass trombones share the greatest number of similarities of any of the doubling combinations discussed in this book, but their differences must be taken into account if you are to perform successfully on both instruments.

The tenor and bass trombones share the same slide positions with the exceptions of the additional possibilities created by the second valve on the bass trombone. Proficient tenor trombonists could pick up a bass trombone and immediately play the correct notes without any training on the larger instrument; this is what many high school and college students do when asked to play bass trombone. The result in such scenarios is predictable: the correct notes are played, but a characteristic bass trombone sound is not achieved, and often with poor intonation due to the student failing to address differences between the two instruments.

The bass trombone has a larger bore and bell than the tenor trombone, but this does not automatically yield the darker and broader sound desired from the bass trombone. A bigger and fuller airstream is required in order to fill the larger instrument so the sound is not only dark but also centered, with lots of core. Some people that play both bass trombone and tuba will even say the air requirements are greater for the bass trombone—an observation which should alert the tenor trombonist that developing an ability to move more air efficiently will be necessary in order to succeed as a bass trombone doubler.

A bass trombone mouthpiece must have a deeper cup and probably a wider diameter than for a tenor trombone. The larger mouthpiece requires a slight difference in the development and use of the facial musculature than that of the tenor trombone. While the same mouthpiece might fit in both receivers, the desired sound will not be achieved unless a larger mouthpiece is used for the bass trombone.

The second valve on the bass trombone must be mastered. This will be discussed in greater detail later in the chapter; suffice it to say for now that you must learn not only the additional fingerings made possible by the second valve, but also the precise locations of the slide positions when the second valve is engaged, both alone (when applicable) and in combination with the first valve. Even the slide positions which are the same as those on the tenor trombone will differ slightly in their precise placement on the bass.

While the doubler on multiple low brass instruments should strive to have approximately the same tonal range on every instrument, each instrument yields its best sound in a particular part of the tonal range. For the bass trombone, this is, unsurprisingly, the lower register. What this means for the player is not so much a change in technique as a change in emphasis, with the low register receiving the attention and effort given to the middle and upper registers on the tenor trombone. This low register focus on the bass trombone can bring with it a *slight* decline in the quality of sound and response in the upper register on the bass trombone relative to the tenor. While you should strive to have a beautiful tone throughout the range on every instrument you play, the cultivation of a pleasing sound in each instrument's primary register is of paramount importance. If you are going to double on the bass trombone, your low range needs to sound great.

Sound Concept

Whether the bass trombone is your primary or secondary instrument, one of the worst mistakes is producing an uncharacteristic timbre sometimes unaffectionately described as the "tuba on a stick" sound—an unfocused, dumpy sound lacking brilliance and direction. This is caused by using an airstream that is too slow and diffuse—a manner of blowing which might be appropriate for the euphonium or tuba but not for a trombone of any kind. This problem can be compounded by using equipment that is too large, which will be addressed shortly.

Develop a sound concept for the bass trombone that is a lower and deeper extension of the tenor trombone sound, rather than something entirely new. Listening to live performances and recordings of great bass trombonists helps with this, as does section and ensemble playing. When playing bass trombone in a trombone section or ensemble, seek to emulate the tenor trombone's clearer and brighter timbre. (Tenor trombonists, in turn, should try to capture some of the richness of sound characteristic of the bass trombone.) This facilitates a dark, rich bass trombone sound which nevertheless still sounds like a *trombone*, as it should.

Intonation

The tenor and bass trombones share the same fundamental pitch, slide positions (except those with the second valve), and overtone series, so the tuning tendencies of the two instruments are very similar. The tenor-to-bass double is therefore easy to manage in terms of learning slide positions and necessary tuning adjustments. The primary intonation difficulties a tenor trombonist will encounter with the bass trombone lie in two areas: upper register, and the second valve.

While the low range expectations for bass trombonists exceed those for tenor trombonists by an octave or more, the upper range expectations are reduced by only a fifth or so. A strong and functional high register is needed on the bass trombone, and given the larger dimensions of the instrument, players with weaker embouchures will tend to play flat and with a weak sound in the upper part of the range. This is solved by the inclusion of high register exercises in regular fundamentals work on the bass trombone, as well as study or performance materials which explore that part of the range. Strengthening the high register on bass trombone will not only improve the tone quality and pitch of that range on the bass, but might yield similar benefits for your tenor playing as well.

The other intonation problem common to tenor-to-bass doublers occurs when using the second valve. While the slide position adjustments for using the F-attachment on the bass are essentially the same as those for the tenor, and those for using the second valve alone are very similar, the positions with both valves engaged are significantly longer—so much so that the instrument has only five positions when using both valves. You must make a conscious effort to locate these positions with the assistance of a tuner but primarily using your *ear*, and then actively and systematically work to master the accurate placement of these positions using fundamental exercises, scale and arpeggio studies, and other materials. Figure 2.1 illustrates the approximate relative locations of the different slide positions on the bass trombone.

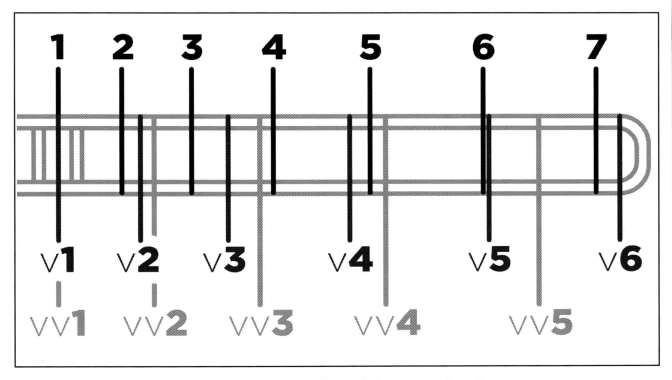

Figure 2.1: Bass trombone slide position locations

NOTE: Slide positions are not equidistant from one another
Numbers across the top = Tenor trombone positions with no valve engaged
v (number) = Positions with one valve engaged
vv (number) = Positions with both valves engaged

The Low Brass Player's Guide to Doubling

Every slide is different, so even the open and F-attachment positions which are familiar from the tenor trombone might not be in precisely the same place on the bass trombone. Treat each slide position as a broad area rather than a fixed spot, and always let your ear guide the placement of each note.

Low Register Articulation

One common error among tenor trombone students—both while playing the tenor and while doubling on bass—is forcing lower notes to speak by using a harder articulation. This often causes response problems, and the player typically tries again with a hard, even explosive articulation. This rarely helps, as the extra force simply causes the lips to separate further and the note still does not speak. The operative error is a faulty concept which confuses the *volume* of air with the *intensity* with which that air is blown through the lips and instrument. The lower register on all brass instruments requires a greater volume of air than the higher register, but combining that with a forceful articulation will lead to the already looser embouchure being blown apart by the momentarily greater air pressure. The solution may seem counterintuitive: tongue more softly in the lower register. With the jaw lowered and the lips already held quite loosely, only a light disruption of the airstream is required to produce a clear articulation. Besides, with the tongue already having to move somewhat farther from its resting position to the articulation point due to the larger oral cavity shape, the softer articulation eliminates unnecessary effort.

A different articulation problem occurs when the player, even when tonguing softly, has difficulty getting a clear initial attack in the lower range because the airflow being released into the instrument is insufficient. Tonguing very softly on the upper lip (rather than behind the upper teeth) can facilitate greater airflow while playing articulated passages below pedal B-flat, even when used only on the initial note of a passage. This technique does not work in every situation and must be used with great care, as it may cause the "explosive tonguing" error and in a worse fashion than when tonguing normally. However, when used correctly it can lead to slightly improved response on pedal tones.

Choosing a Mouthpiece

As with all choices of doubling mouthpieces, the primary question is whether you will use the same mouthpiece rim on both instruments or choose a mouthpiece with a wider diameter for the bass trombone. Using the same rim on both instruments can be advantageous because it minimizes the change in the use of the embouchure musculature from one instrument to the next. Provided that you use a deep cup and an appropriate backbore for the bass trombone, you can produce a characteristic bass trombone sound with this kind of setup despite the narrow diameter. However, using a tenor trombone rim on bass trombone can limit flexibility and response, particularly in the lowest part of the range, and thus additional practice will be needed to overcome this limitation. Using a more conventional bass trombone mouthpiece with a wider diameter yields a characteristic sound on the bass as well as ready response, at least with practice, but such a mouthpiece change might increase the amount of time needed to master the bass trombone double. Maintaining playing ability on both instruments also requires just a bit more effort when using two entirely different mouthpieces than when using the same rim on both. Neither option leads to entirely trouble-free doubling with regard to mouthpieces and either solution is workable with sufficient practice.

If you decide to use an entirely different mouthpiece on the bass trombone than on the tenor, resist the urge to use the biggest mouthpiece you can find. Some players, including tenor-to-bass doublers, are able to do quite well using very large mouthpieces on bass trombone, but moving to the biggest sizes too early will only exacerbate the timbre and intonation problems discussed earlier in this chapter. A mouthpiece with a cup diameter of approximately 27mm, a mid-range size from most manufacturers, will be sufficient as a first bass trombone mouthpiece and might even serve for your entire doubling career. Moving to a larger size might be desirable after you have developed greater strength and skill on the bass trombone, but doing so too early will hinder rather than help your development as a bass trombonist.

Choosing an Instrument

The tendency to think "bigger is better" with the bass trombone can also cause difficulties with instrument choice. While pricing is often a primary consideration when choosing an instrument for doubling, you should carefully consider certain characteristics, particularly when beginning your career as a bass trombonist.

Consider the bore size. The standard bass trombone bore is .562 inch, but dual-bore slides with a .562 inch upper leg and a .578 inch lower leg have become increasingly common, and one occasionally encounters even larger sizes. While strong and experienced players might do quite well with a larger instrument, the tenor-to-bass doubler who is just starting out will likely find such an instrument difficult to manage, at least without producing the dreaded "tuba on a stick" timbre. For your first bass trombone, a traditional .562 inch bore instrument will almost certainly be best.

A related consideration is bell size. While most bass trombone bells are 9.5 inches in diameter, 10 inch bells are also common, and a few instruments are made with 10.5 inch bells. As with larger bore sizes, there are players who do very well with larger bells, but those new to the bass trombone will probably be most successful with a 9.5 inch bell. In the hands of a strong player, larger bells can sound quite good in a large ensemble playing at loud volumes but are less effective at softer volumes or in solo and chamber music situations. Because of this, the largest bells tend to have very limited application. The 9.5 inch bell facilitates a softer and more compact sound when needed while also allowing you to open up when louder volumes are needed.

A more complex decision is the choice of valves and valve systems. Practically all commercially available models of tenor trombone have either no valve or only one valve which lowers the first-position fundamental pitch to F. Despite the availability of different valve types and wraps, the function of the valve is the same on virtually all tenor trombones. When purchasing a bass trombone, you must choose whether to purchase an instrument with one or two valves. The majority of available literature for the bass trombone can be played with only an F-attachment. The second valve adds only three additional notes to the instrument's tonal range (see figure 2.2) but the various low-register fingering options added by the second valve greatly enhance technical facility in that range. Those concerned with the weight of the second valve can consider instruments on which that valve is removable, thus using the instrument in its heaviest configuration only when needed.

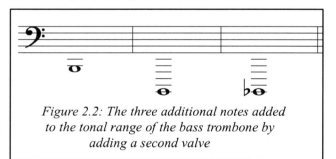

Figure 2.2: The three additional notes added to the tonal range of the bass trombone by adding a second valve

Choosing a double-valve instrument over a single-valve one is a relatively easy decision; deciding on the configuration and tuning of the second valve is less so. The first consideration here is the choice between bass trombones with dependent and independent configurations. In the dependent configuration (see figure 2.3) the second valve is mounted on the first valve's tubing, so the second valve can only be used when the first valve is engaged. In the independent configuration (see figure 2.4), the second valve is mounted on the main body of the instrument so the second valve can be used either independently or in combination with the first. Each of these configurations has its advantages: the independent configuration provides more fingering options, but the instrument

Figure 2.3: Bass trombone with dependent rotary valves

Figure 2.4: Bass trombone with independent Thayer valves

might be a bit less free-blowing because you are always blowing against the resistance of two valves (the slight bends or constrictions in the tubing associated with most valve designs cause a slight disruption in the airflow even when the valve is not engaged); dependent instruments might be more free-blowing but present fewer fingering options. The choice between these two configurations is thus a choice between different sets of strengths and weaknesses, and is entirely at your discretion.

While the first valve on most bass trombones is an F-attachment like that on most tenor trombones, the tuning of the second valve is less standardized. The most common tuning option when both valves are engaged has the first-position fundamental pitch of D (see figure 2.5); independent bass trombones with this tuning will have a fundamental pitch of G-flat when the second valve is

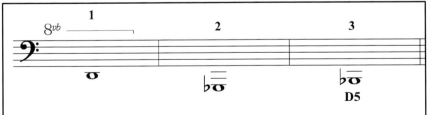

Figure 2.5: Two valve independent bass trombone - first tuning option
1 = Fundamental with both valves engaged
2 = Fundamental with just the second valve engaged
3 = Alternate position for pedal B-flat with both valves engaged

used alone. I find this tuning to be preferable partly because it is most common (and therefore much of the available study material is geared toward players using it), and because it provides a useful alternate position for pedal B-flat in the lowest position with both valves engaged. Still, some players prefer to have the second valve tuned to G with E-flat produced with the two valves combined (see figure 2.6), and there are some more exotic tunings available such as having the second valve tuned to a quarter-tone between G and G-flat, and even having an independent D attachment where the second valve alone lowers the fundamental pitch to D1 and the two valves combined lower the fundamental by a full octave. While these latter options (and still others not mentioned here) have their proponents, the G-flat/D tuning (option one above) is most common and therefore recommended, at least when first beginning bass trombone study.

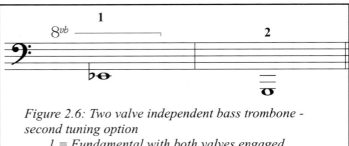

Figure 2.6: Two valve independent bass trombone - second tuning option
1 = Fundamental with both valves engaged
2 = Fundamental with just the second valve engaged

You must also choose between types of valves when purchasing a bass trombone. Tenor trombonists will already be familiar with the variety of valve designs on the market, but the choice of valve type has perhaps a greater effect on the sound and response of the bass trombone simply because there are two valves rather than one. While traditional rotary valves are still available and are often the lightest, least expensive, and lowest-maintenance option, axial-flow (or "Thayer") valves and various other proprietary valve types are very popular among bass trombonists, as these newer designs promise less constriction than traditional rotary valves. Ergonomics and weight also must be considered; each valve type alters the weight of the instrument differently and the tubing wrap required by each is different, thus altering the instrument's balance. Traditional rotary valves are usually the most lightweight option, but you might choose to manage a bit of extra weight in order to enjoy a more free-blowing playing experience. While each available valve design promises a particular set of improvements in response and feel, the difference between these is mostly limited to the player's subjective experience; listeners are rarely able to hear a difference between valve types on otherwise similar instruments. Choose the valve type that you find the most comfortable to hold and to play, or perhaps the one that is the most cost-effective.

Improving Ergonomics and Balance

While the bass trombone has the same amount of tubing on the main body of the instrument as the tenor trombone and a nearly identical holding position, its larger bore and bell and the second valve increase the weight of the instrument and in some cases cause it to be poorly balanced. This makes the physical efficiency and relaxation needed for great playing particularly difficult to establish and maintain. Happily, there are adjustments can be made and exercises that you can use to eliminate or effectively cope with these difficulties.

Perhaps the greatest difficulty in holding and playing the bass trombone lies in the left hand grip. The earliest double-valve instruments were designed so that both valves were operated by the left thumb (see figure 2.3); on more recent models the first valve is operated by the thumb and the second valve by the middle finger (see figure 2.4). While this setup enhances dexterity in operating the valves, it also necessitates that you support and balance the weight of the instrument almost entirely with the third and fourth fingers of the left hand. This can cause discomfort in the left hand and wrist, and might lead to supporting part of the instrument's weight with the right hand. This latter fault is especially egregious, as it hampers slide movement and can eventually cause the handslide to bend out of alignment. Players experiencing such problems must take steps to alleviate symptoms in the left hand and wrist so that a correct holding and playing position is comfortably maintained.

Figure 2.7: Alternate left hand position

An easy solution is a slight modification of the left hand grip (see figure 2.7). While most players hold the bass trombone using the same grip as one would use on a tenor, with second, third, and fourth fingers underneath the first slide brace (the second finger operating the second valve paddle), moving the second finger to the other side of the brace allows the third finger to rest against the brace, thus improving the balance of the two weight-bearing fingers. While adjusting the position of the second valve paddle may be necessary in order to make this position workable, many instruments are designed so this paddle can be repositioned by the player without a trip to the repair

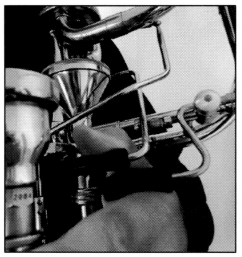

Figure 2.8: Edwards bullet brace

shop. Even if the assistance of a repair technician is necessary, the adjustment should be simple and inexpensive. While this modified grip might feel strange at first, players using it report that the weird feeling passes quickly, and the improved comfort when playing is well worth any initial disturbance.

A costlier solution is to attach a device which causes the instrument's weight to be supported less by the left wrist and hand and more by the larger muscles of the forearm. While such devices have been produced by several manufacturers, most can be broadly classified under two types. The first is a post which attaches either to the first bell brace or the handslide receiver and extends to a position where it rests between the left thumb and forefinger (see figure 2.8). The second is a larger, padded metal plate which also attaches to the first bell brace and then rests across the back of the left hand (see figure 2.9). With both of these designs, the fingers of the left hand are freed of all weight bearing requirements, with larger muscle groups supporting the instrument's weight. Most of these devices can be attached to the instrument without heat or soldering and can be removed or repositioned as needed.

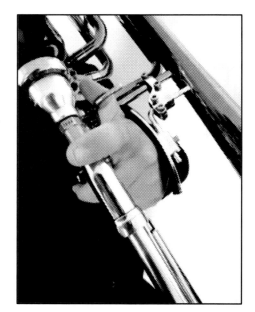

Figure 2.9: Rath hand brace

Another type of device promising ergonomic improvement consists of a peg or stick which attaches to the instrument and then rests on the player's chair, in a harness worn by the player, or even on the floor (see figure 2.10). While a few manufacturers make competing products, the most common of these is the ERGObone. When configured with the support peg resting on the chair or floor, the player is responsible for supporting practically none of the instrument's weight—only for providing balance. When the harness is used, the weight is borne by the legs, back, and chest, with none supported by the arms. Devices like the ERGObone do have certain limitations. Mute changes are sometimes difficult or awkward and movement is somewhat restricted, particularly with regard to minute adjustments of the mouthpiece and embouchure. Still, if

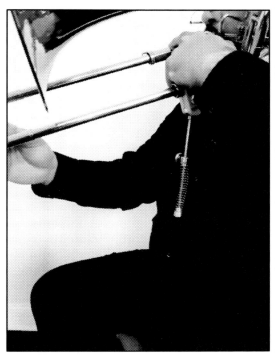

Figure 2.10: ERGObone

you are seeking nearly complete release from supporting the instrument's weight, devices like the ERGObone do provide that relief.

None of these suggestions are a complete replacement for making sure you are in the best physical shape possible. A moderate strength training regimen, with the left arm perhaps being particularly targeted, is extremely helpful. Even when steps are taken to improve ergonomics and balance, the bass trombone remains a heavy and unwieldy instrument. Strengthening the body is simply another tool for enabling efficient and comfortable playing, and you will enjoy better overall health to boot!

Suggested Practice and Performance Literature

The following materials, combined with regular use of a fundamentals routine such as that described above and diligent practice of scales and arpeggios, will further your development as a tenor-to-bass trombone doubler. The Aharoni and Raph books are particularly designed to increase familiarity with the double-valve instrument. The Snedecor targets the development of facility in the extreme low register, while the others remain mostly in the bass trombone's cash register (i.e. low, but not at the very bottom). While complete parts are always preferred to excerpt books for practice of orchestral repertoire, the Rosin/Pleyer volume is quite thorough and more portable than a folder full of parts. Playing the Arban exercises one and two octaves below the written ranges will do much to promote facility in the low register. Regular use of the Vining book will promote correct use of the body when playing, particularly with regard to air movement. The solo repertoire listed should be accessible to doublers with limited experience, exercising the instrument's low register while also exploiting the warm, rich sound the instrument is capable of producing throughout its tonal range.

Method Books

Aharoni, Eliezer - *New Method for the Modern Bass Trombone*

Arban, Jean-Baptiste, edited by Joseph Alessi and Dr. Brian Bowman - *Complete Method for Trombone & Euphonium*

Bordogni, Giulio Marco, arranged and edited by Allen Ostrander - *Melodious Etudes for Bass Trombone*

Grigoriev, Boris, edited by Allen Ostrander - *24 Studies for Bass Trombone or Trombone with F-attachment*

Kopprasch, Georg, edited by Dr. Jerry Young - *Sixty Etudes for Tuba Op. 5*

Raph, Alan - *The Double Valve Bass Trombone*

Remington, Emory, prepared and edited by Donald Hunsberger - *The Remington Warm-Up Studies*

Rosin, Armin and Eberhard Pleyer - *Test Pieces for Orchestral Auditions: Trombone*

Schlossberg, Max, edited by C.K. Schlossberg - *Daily Drills and Technical Studies for Trombone*

Snedecor, Phil - *Low Etudes for Tuba*

Vining, David - *The Breathing Book for Bass Trombone*

Solo Repertoire

Dossett, Tom - *Trilogy for Bass Trombone*

Galliard, Johann Ernst, edited by Micah Everett - *Six Sonatas for Bass Trombone and Keyboard*

Hindemith, Paul - *Drei leichte Stücke*

Hoffman, Earl - *Trigger Treat*

Jacob, Gordon - *Cameos*

Lieb, Richard - *Concertino Basso*

McCarty, Patrick - *Sonata for Bass Trombone*

Raph, Alan - *Rock*

Semler-Collery, Jules - *Barcarolle et Chanson Bachique*

Appendix C: Bass Trombone Resources

Targeted Fundamentals 135

Fingering Charts 141

Overtone Series Charts 145

Chapter 3: Bass Trombonists Doubling on Tenor Trombone

At first glance, this chapter might seem superfluous. After all, most bass trombonists began their musical lives on tenor trombone, so to add a tenor trombone double after switching to bass trombone is not as much an exploration of a new instrument as it is becoming reacquainted with an old one. Furthermore, many of the suggestions in this chapter are simply the reverse of those presented in the previous chapter. Nevertheless, there are bass trombonists who started on euphonium, tuba, or some other instrument and thus never played the tenor, as well as players who went directly to the bass trombone from a student-line tenor and have never tried to play the latter instrument at a higher level; both of these groups will benefit from this chapter.

With regard to notes and fingerings, playing the tenor trombone simply entails subtracting one or both valves, with the remaining available slide positions being the same as those on the bass trombone (with subtle differences in the precise location of each position). The holding position is identical except that the left middle finger is able to help support the instrument instead of operating a valve lever. This chapter will focus on timbre, intonation, and equipment selection, since these issues are more likely to cause problems for the bass-to-tenor doubler than fingerings or holding position.

A Suggestion Before Beginning: High Range Development

The tenor trombone will lend a certain ease of production to your high register when compared to playing the same range on the bass trombone, but is unlikely to automatically add notes to your high range. In preparation for taking up the tenor trombone, practice the high register on the bass with great diligence. It requires greater strength and efficiency to produce high notes on the larger equipment, so if your high register on the bass trombone is already good, that same register on the tenor can become *great*, perhaps very quickly.

Sound Concept

As a bass trombonist, your primary challenge with regard to a tenor trombone sound concept is to avoid producing a sound that is too dark and tubby or out of control as the result of overblowing the instrument. The characteristic sound of the bass and tenor trombones should be similar, with the tenor trombone sound a more compact version of the bass. The tenor trombone must be blown with an airstream that is similar to that of the bass trombone but smaller and more focused, with slightly less air. Perhaps the easiest way to achieve this is to think of a trumpet-like sound when playing the tenor. Thinking of a sound that is brighter than that which is really desired can be a helpful way to avoid the opposite error of playing with a timbre that is too dark and tubby. Of course, a conceptual shortcut like this is no substitute for listening to and playing with great tenor trombonists, always seeking to emulate their sounds. One of the best ways to improve is to play with people who are better than you.

In some respects, the mention of a single tenor trombone sound is misleading, as the big sound favored by orchestral players is markedly different from the more compact sound that predominates in the jazz and commercial realms. While the approach described above works in either instance, the latter sound is a greater departure from the bass trombone timbre than the former. Much of this difference is also addressed by changes in equipment, which will be discussed shortly.

Intonation

The error of playing with a tubby sound can also cause the pitch to be flat. To fix this problem, cultivate a tenor trombone sound concept as described above and use a mouthpiece with a cup and backbore appropriate for the tenor trombone—your bass mouthpiece will be too deep. Once these issues are addressed, the primary intonation challenge is becoming familiar with the tenor trombone slide positions. While all B-flat trombones share the same overtone series, open slide positions, and basic intonation tendencies, every slide is slightly different and the locations of the various positions will differ slightly from one instrument to the next. Bass trombonists might be especially surprised to discover that small-bore tenor trombone slides can be slightly *longer* than bass trombone slides, given the smaller distance between the pairs of slide tubes on one end and the two sides of the bell section on the other. The additional length of the small-bore slide is particularly felt at the end of the slide. Bass trombonists accustomed to using valves to avoid the long positions will find accurate placement of those positions in the absence of valves to be especially challenging. This illustrates the importance of conceiving of slide positions more as areas than as particular spots, as this concept gives you the flexibility needed to easily move between different slides. The regular practice of targeted fundamental exercises and scales on every instrument also helps ensure accurate tuning and slide placement regardless of the instrument being played.

Choosing an Instrument or Instruments

Whereas most bass trombonists can manage very well with a single instrument, tenor trombonists often cannot. The smaller-bore and usually valveless instruments preferred in the jazz and commercial realms are rarely appropriate for performing in large orchestras, concert bands, or even in solo and chamber ensemble settings, where the sound of a large-bore instrument is expected. If you are seeking a diverse tenor trombone career, you will need to purchase at least two instruments to satisfy the specific musical needs of any given situation. Happily, tenor trombones—particularly those without F-attachments—are less expensive than bass trombones, so even if two instruments are needed, you need not break the bank in order to purchase them.

For most classical playing, a .547 inch bore with an 8.5 inch bell is considered standard. Larger bells, dual-bore handslides, and even .562 inch handslides (essentially bass trombone slides) are available if desired, though the bass-to-tenor doubler might find that these larger options cause difficulty in achieving the desired tenor trombone sound. While smaller instruments are appropriate for certain situations (such as performing eighteenth century orchestral repertoire), showing up for a classical gig with a smaller instrument, unless instructed beforehand to do so, would be unwise. An F-attachment is expected, though the type of valve chosen is at the discretion of the player. Modular instruments can be fitted with a straight gooseneck which can be used in situations not requiring the F-attachment; removal of the valve section changes the *sound* of the instrument very little and doing so reduces the *weight* of the instrument quite a bit, making this a desirable option for some players.

The instruments commonly used in jazz and commercial playing are not as standardized, but are usually smaller than those used in classical playing. Bore sizes range from .480 inch to .525 inch and bell sizes from seven inches to eight inches, with lead players often preferring the smaller sizes and players in more aggressive genres leaning toward the larger ones. F-attachments are not always available on instruments in these sizes, and in any case are rarely needed. While a few soloists have even begun using .547 inch bore instruments for jazz work, the mellow sound produced by the large-bore instrument will not always cut through sufficiently in a big band situation. My preference is to use a .508 inch bore instrument with an eight inch bell for this type of playing, and this is what I suggest for bass-to-tenor doublers looking for a smaller tenor. As one who plays larger instruments much more frequently than smaller ones, I find this size yields the timbre I want with a somewhat easier transition between instruments than I experienced with a smaller jazz horn. Using a more open leadpipe and a mouthpiece with a relatively open backbore can further ease the bass trombonist's transition to a small-bore tenor trombone.

Some readers might wonder whether a .525 inch bore instrument could serve as a single "do everything" instrument for tenor trombone doubling, eliminating the need to purchase and maintain two instruments for tenor trombone playing. There are certainly a number of situations where a .525 inch bore would serve very well, but it usually fails to adequately serve the purpose of either of the two instruments it is intended to replace. My recommendation in most cases remains to use a .547 inch bore instrument for classical playing and a .508 inch bore for commercial work. Purchasing a .525 inch bore instrument *in addition to these* for use in applicable situations is certainly appropriate, but not as a *replacement* for either.

Choosing Mouthpieces

Since two instruments are often needed for tenor trombone doubling, two mouthpieces will almost certainly also be needed. While the process of mouthpiece selection will be similar for both instruments, given the distinctive timbres desired from each, I will discuss mouthpiece selection for large-bore and small-bore instruments separately.

The sound expected from the large-bore tenor trombone has become even bigger, darker, and broader in recent years, and the corresponding trend is to use larger mouthpieces. Bass-to-tenor doublers should take care to choose a mouthpiece for the large-bore tenor that is deep enough to yield the desired sound but not so deep that it becomes too much like a bass trombone sound. A good approach is to choose the biggest mouthpiece which will facilitate the desired timbre as well as provide ease in upper register playing—perhaps a mouthpiece approximately the depth of a Bach 4G. You could go a bit shallower (5G) and *maybe* a bit deeper (3G) without difficulty, but going too far beyond that range is inadvisable, for both timbre and pitch considerations.

Choosing a mouthpiece for the small-bore tenor might be easier, as there is little danger of selecting and using what is essentially a small bass trombone mouthpiece. Nevertheless, choosing the smallest mouthpiece for the small-bore tenor trombone can lead to difficulties with transitioning between bass and tenor; a mouthpiece that is on the larger end of those still appropriate for the small-bore instrument will probably be best. The Bach 6.5AL is a good starting place because it is shallow enough to facilitate the bright timbre needed for lead playing, and deep enough to produce a more mellow sound for section playing in jazz ensembles or even those orchestral works which require the use of smaller equipment. A larger mouthpiece will almost certainly be inappropriate for the small

The Low Brass Player's Guide to Doubling

bore tenor; a smaller one can be used if desired, but exceedingly shallow mouthpieces will not be as versatile, and bass-to-tenor doublers in particular might find them difficult to play.

Regarding mouthpiece diameter, there are arguments in favor of using a single mouthpiece rim for all playing, as well as for using standard diameters for each mouthpiece. While playing the tenor trombones using your bass trombone rim might ease the transition between mouthpieces, achieving the necessary focused tone can be difficult with such a setup, particularly on the small-bore instrument. At the same time, bass trombonists accustomed to a wide-diameter mouthpiece might find a standard small-bore tenor mouthpiece to be uncomfortably confining. A possible compromise would be to use a wide-diameter tenor trombone rim on both the large-bore and small-bore tenors—something smaller than your bass trombone rim but not uncomfortably tiny. All of these approaches have pros and cons, so ultimately you are responsible for experimenting with different mouthpieces and finding the one that works best.

Clefs

While bass trombonists rarely encounter tenor and alto clefs, both of these are regularly used by tenor trombonists, so bass-to-tenor doublers will need to increase their clef reading abilities in order to be successful. Reading by interval, starting on a known pitch and proceeding from there by considering the intervals between notes, is a very helpful approach to clef reading in the early stages; singing clef studies using solfège is also an excellent tool.

Developing greater mastery of tenor clef yields the added benefit of being able to read music written in treble clef, with the sounding pitch a major ninth lower than the written pitch. Trombone music using this transposition is rare in the United States but standard fare in certain contexts, particularly works influenced by the British brass band tradition. This transposition also makes works for trumpet and other instruments with the same transposition available to you. Consult Chapter 5 for a more extended treatment of this particular skill.

While it is not technically a different clef, bass-to-tenor doublers might want to devote some practice time to reading ledger lines above the bass clef staff. Tenor and alto clefs are common in classical genres but rare in the jazz and commercial realms, and lead parts in particular can stay well above the staff for the full duration of a chart. While as a bass-to-tenor doubler you might not be the first-call player for a lead book, being prepared for anything means making sure that tenor and alto clefs and high bass clef ledger lines are well in hand.

The Low Brass Player's Guide to Doubling

Suggested Practice and Performance Literature

The technical aims of the Arban and Kopprasch volumes are obvious, as are the purposes of the Rosin/Pleyer excerpts book and of the Blazhevich and Edwards clef studies. The Snidero book serves in a limited fashion as a clef study in addition to a treatise on jazz styling, as it sometimes uses the multiple ledger lines often encountered in jazz ensembles' lead trombone books. The Lafosse books provide useful work on accurate reading and execution; I often wish these books were available in editions for other instruments. Like the similar book mentioned in the previous chapter, the Vining volume promotes correct breathing and use of the body. The solo works listed here are standard fare for young undergraduate tenor trombonists. They are challenging yet accessible and thus quite appropriate for doublers, particularly those just beginning their work on the tenor trombone.

Method Books

Arban, Jean-Baptiste, edited by Joseph Alessi and Dr. Brian Bowman - *Complete Method for Trombone and Euphonium*

Blazhevich, Vladislav, edited by Andrey Kharlamov and Michael Deryugin with annotations by Ward Stare - *School for Trombone in Clefs*

Bordogni, Giulio Marco, annotated and edited by Michael Mulcahy - *Complete Vocalises for Trombone*

Edwards, Brad - *Introductory Studies in Tenor & Alto Clef for Trombone "Before Blazhevich"*

Kopprasch, Georg, edited by Keith Brown - *60 Studies for Trombone* (2 vols.)

Lafosse, André - *School of Sight Reading and Style for Tenor Trombone* (5 vols.)

Remington, Emory, prepared and edited by Donald Hunsberger - *The Remington Warm-Up Studies*

Rosin, Armin and Eberhard Pleyer - *Test Pieces for Orchestral Auditions: Trombone*

Schlossberg, Max, edited by C.K. Schlossberg - *Daily Drills and Technical Studies for Trombone*

Snidero, Jim - *Jazz Conception*

Vining, David - *The Breathing Book for Tenor Trombone*

Solo Repertoire

Barat, J. Ed. - *Andante et Allegro for Trombone and Piano*

Guilmant, Alexandre, arranged by E. Falaguerra - *Morceau Symphonique*

Hasse, Johann Adolph, compiled and edited by Wm. Gower - *Hasse Suite*

Larsson, Lars-Erik – *Concertino, Op. 45 No. 7*

Marcello, Benedetto, edited by Walter Schulz - *Six Sonatas for Violoncello and Continuo*

Pryor, Arthur - *Solos for Trombone*

Rimsky-Korsakov, Nicolai - *Trombone Concerto*

Saint-Saëns, Camille – *Cavatine for Trombone and Piano, Op. 144*

Šulek, Stjepan - *Sonata (Vox Gabrieli) for Trombone and Piano*

Telemann, Georg Philipp, edited by Allen Ostrander and Robert Veyron-Lecroix - *Sonata in F Minor*

Weber, Carl Maria von - *Romance*

Appendix D: Tenor Trombone Resources

Targeted Fundamentals 147

Fingering Chart 150

Overtone Series Chart 152

Chapter 4: Doubling on Two or More Sizes of the Same Instrument

The practice of doubling on small-bore and large-bore tenor trombones is addressed in this chapter. Similar ideas apply to any player who performs on two or more of the same instrument in different sizes, such as 3/4 and 5/4 CC tubas, or American-style and German-style trombones of similar proportions.

The tenor trombone player who aspires to work in both the (broadly-defined) classical and jazz realms will need to play both small-bore and large-bore instruments. In order to do this *well*, you must treat one or the other of these instruments as a double. Trombonists who are primarily classical players that occasionally play a smaller instrument in a jazz ensemble, pit orchestra, or similar setting may be tempted to neglect regular practice on the smaller instrument. After all, both are tenor trombones, share the same slide positions, and may even be played with the same mouthpiece rim. Regular practice on the small-bore instrument is advisable in order to avoid the following problems with air and response, timbre, and tuning.

1. Overblowing the small-bore instrument

This is a common mistake, with the airflow backing up and causing discomfort and response problems due to the aperture being blown apart. While this problem can be mitigated by using a more open leadpipe in the small-bore instrument, the instrument will not respond properly until a more compact airstream is used. This adjustment is relatively easy to master, but some practice is required for it to become both comfortable and automatic. It is not unlike the adjustment made by bass trombonists doubling on tenor trombone, but to a lesser degree.

2. Playing with an uncharacteristic tone on the small-bore instrument

The large-bore player who fails to adjust to the blowing needs of the smaller horn probably also has the big orchestral sound of Mahler and Strauss in mind, which is impossible (and unnecessary) to achieve on a small-bore trombone. In this case, the sound is woofy and uncentered, and response problems are likely. The player needs not only to make the airflow adjustment just mentioned, but also ensure that the sound concept in mind is characteristic for the instrument and genre being played.

The Low Brass Player's Guide to Doubling

3. Poor intonation on the small-bore instrument

While all B-flat trombones share the same slide positions, not all B-flat trombone *slides* are precisely the same length. Smaller-bore instruments in particular tend to have slightly longer slides than larger-bore instruments. The player that does not maintain a working familiarity with the small-bore instrument will tend to place slide positions in familiar locations associated with the larger instrument, resulting in faulty intonation. The solution to this problem is to practice fundamentals regularly on the smaller instrument, with particular emphasis on scale and arpeggio exercises to improve intonation. The player should conceive of each slide position as a broadly defined area, with adjustments easily made according to the needs of the moment.

The difficulties encountered by a small-bore player who only occasionally plays a large-bore instrument are the reverse of those just discussed. The same intonation difficulties will be encountered, though in this case because one is accustomed to a longer slide rather than a shorter one. Instead of overblowing the large-bore instrument, the player will fail to use enough air to fill the larger horn, producing a sound which lacks both volume and core. Failure to properly conceive of the bigger airstream and slightly more relaxed embouchure required by the large instrument could also lead to a bizarre type of overblowing—not of the instrument but of the player's embouchure, in which the player tries to force too much air through a tight aperture rather than relaxing the facial musculature to facilitate playing with a big, warm, and relaxed sound, even at louder volumes.

Tenor trombones of different sizes might share many similarities, but each has subtle peculiarities which must be understood, practiced, and mastered if one is to successfully play both. In other words, these must be conceived of and practiced as separate doubling instruments according to the principles discussed throughout this book. This includes use of Targeted Fundamentals for tenor trombone, which appears in Appendix C, on whichever of the two instruments is the doubling instrument. While the example of playing on tenor trombones of different sizes has been used here because it is common, similar requirements will apply to any performer playing two or more versions of the same instrument. Do not assume that because you can play one very well you will automatically be able to play the other well. Every instrument you play regularly must be practiced diligently if you hope to succeed as a doubler.

Chapter 5: Trombonists Doubling on Euphonium

The euphonium is a common secondary instrument for both tenor and bass trombonists, and is usually easy to learn. While this double rarely generates much freelance performing work, it can be a boon to your teaching because gaining mastery of a valved brass instrument enables you to teach all of the brasses at some level and all of the low brasses in particular. This certainly increases employment opportunities as a teacher; my euphonium skills were a vital part of attaining two university positions. The euphonium is a rewarding double from a musical perspective—its cello-like role in the concert band often makes playing euphonium parts in that setting more enjoyable than playing trombone parts. The euphonium plays a central role in British-style brass bands, a tradition which has spawned an exciting and accessible solo repertoire for the instrument. While rare, the euphonium is occasionally used in orchestral, jazz, and popular music.

Prologue: Take the Euphonium Seriously!

Trombonists should not underestimate the challenges in learning to play the euphonium competently. It is relatively easy to produce the correct pitches on the euphonium with a minimal investment of time and effort, but to develop a full, rich, beautiful euphonium sound takes practice. Cultivate a characteristic euphonium sound and you will be a far more successful doubler.

Choosing an Instrument

The euphonium player has fewer available equipment choices than the trombonist, with fewer reputable makers manufacturing instruments and fewer instruments available from those makers. Some manufacturers offer modular options, but the parts are rarely interchangeable once selected. The most important question is whether to choose a compensating or non-compensating instrument (the selection of a four-valve instrument over a three-valve one should be a given). An inherent flaw in all valve systems is that when valves are used in combination, the resulting tubing length is too short to produce the desired notes in tune. The more valves added, the greater the discrepancy between the length of tubing used and the length needed to yield an in tune note. The compensating system compensates for this by rerouting the air through additional short lengths of tubing when certain valve combinations are used. The four-valve compensating euphonium (see figure 5.1) is the most common today, with extra lengths of tubing coming into play when any or all of the first three

 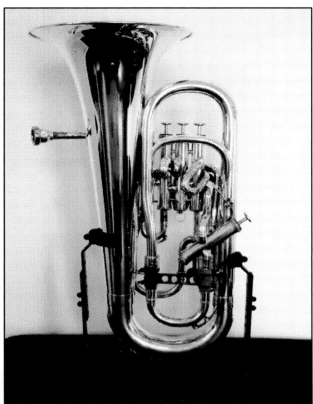

Figure 5.1: Compensating euphonium (front and rear view)

valves are used in combination with the fourth. This corrects many (not all) of the inherent pitch discrepancies when playing low-register notes using the fourth valve, and makes the instrument fully chromatic (Low B and Pedal B are not possible on non-compensating instruments - see figure 5.2).

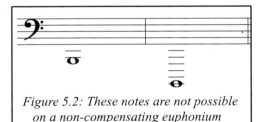

Figure 5.2: These notes are not possible on a non-compensating euphonium

Non-compensating euphoniums (see figure 5.3) lack this additional tubing and its accompanying pitch correction, which necessitates that low-register fingerings be modified to manually correct their sharpness. Occasionally a fifth valve is added to non-compensating instruments, which provides additional pitch correction possibilities and restores the missing notes.

Aside from the tuning in the low register, there is no inherent superiority of compensating instruments over non-compensating ones, and the extra weight and expense of the compensating instrument is an argument in favor of non-compensating models. At the time of writing, purchase prices for the top compensating instruments are approaching $10,000, while quality non-compensating instruments can be purchased for less than half that amount. The compensating

Figure 5.3: Non-compensating euphonium (front and rear view)

instrument is the standard for those pursuing solo and chamber opportunities as well as regular professional employment (such as in military bands); a non-compensating instrument will very likely suffice for those who are taking up this double only for teaching and occasional performing. Most players would argue that the compensating instrument is superior (though a few have a decided preference for the non-compensating instrument), but given the very limited remunerative possibilities for performing euphonium players (at least in the United States), you might at least consider non-compensating models. In fact, the choice of mouthpiece might be even more important than the choice of instrument in enabling you to produce the best euphonium sound possible. To summarize, the answer to the question of which instrument to purchase is the best one you can afford.

Choosing a Mouthpiece

Tone quality is usually the biggest obstacle to trombone players becoming skilled doublers on the euphonium, the tendency being to produce a tone that is excessively bright and focused (like that of the trombone) rather than warm and expansive. This problem must be addressed primarily by the player independent of equipment, first by developing a correct sound concept and then by slight adjustments to the airstream; however, equipment—especially the choice of mouthpiece—does play a role in realizing the correct tone.

A tenor trombonist should use a euphonium mouthpiece that has the same rim or one very similar to his trombone mouthpiece, but with a cup that is deeper and fuller. The larger cup size facilitates the greater warmth and depth of sound desired from the euphonium, but since the euphonium and tenor trombone share essentially the same core tonal range, there is no need to introduce a change in rim size when taking on this particular double. There are now several mouthpiece lines specifically designed and marketed as euphonium mouthpieces, as a category distinct from trombone mouthpieces (this has not always been the case). A mouthpiece from one of these lines with a rim similar to your trombone mouthpiece would be a good place to begin.

Mouthpiece selection for bass trombonists doubling on euphonium is not as straightforward. Players using smaller bass trombone mouthpieces might find that those mouthpieces work reasonably well on the euphonium, though moving to a slightly shallower cup might be necessary. Some of the euphonium mouthpiece lines mentioned in the previous paragraph include models with diameters equal to those of smaller bass trombone mouthpieces, which might also be an effective option. Those that play larger bass trombone mouthpieces will have to decide whether to use custom or screw-rim mouthpieces pairing that wide rim with a cup more appropriate for the euphonium, or to use an entirely different mouthpiece for euphonium doubling. The former option will lead to an easier transition between instruments, but producing a characteristic sound in the upper register might be more difficult. The latter option will yield the characteristic sound more easily, but with more time and effort needed for skill development and maintenance.

Euphoniums are manufactured with the small and large-shank mouthpiece receivers common to trombones, as well as a medium or European shank which is rarer but still used on a few instruments. Shank size is not nearly as important as cup diameter or depth when considering mouthpieces, but be aware that not all makes and models of mouthpieces are available with all three shanks. When considering and purchasing a mouthpiece make sure you choose one which will fit your instrument's receiver.

Fingerings

Mastering euphonium fingerings is a fairly simple task—the different valve combinations

The Low Brass Player's Guide to Doubling

correspond to trombone slide positions as in the following chart. The fingering combinations using the fourth valve differ depending on whether you have a non-compensating or compensating instrument.

Tenor Trombone with F Attachment Slide Positions	Bass Trombone (F/G-flat/D) Slide Positions	Non-Compensating Euphonium Fingerings	Compensating Euphonium Fingerings
1	1	Open	Open
2	2	2	2
3	3	1	1
4	4	1-2, or 3	1-2, or 3
5	5, or G♭1	2-3	2-3
6, or F1	6, F1, or G♭2	4, or 1-3	4, or 1-3
7, or F2	7, F2, or G♭3	2-4, or 1-2-3	2-4, or 1-2-3
F3	F3, or G♭4	1-4, or 1-2-4	1-4
F4	F4, G♭5, or D1	2-3-4	1-2-4
F5	F5, G♭6, or D2	1-3-4	2-3-4
F6	F6, or D3	1-2-3-4	1-3-4
Not Present	D4	Not Present	1-2-3-4

Thinking of euphonium fingerings by way of trombone slide position equivalents is normal at first and should be encouraged, but seek to eliminate this intermediate step as quickly as possible. Practicing easy to moderately difficult music that has already been mastered on the trombone can help with the development of correct fingerings. Fingering exercises, scales, and arpeggios with a metronome should be part of your daily practice.

Holding Position

An important part of developing finger dexterity and agility—and overall freedom and efficiency in playing euphonium—is holding the instrument properly and using the correct finger position (see figure 5.4). As is the case with the trombone, the weight of the euphonium should be supported entirely with the left arm. Care should be taken to raise the mouthpiece to the level of the embouchure, rather than hunching over (see figure 5.5) in order to reach the mouthpiece in a lower position. In other words, bring the mouthpiece to you, not you to the mouthpiece.

Figure 5.4: Correct holding position with the ERGObrass brace

Figure 5.5: Incorrect holding position: hunched over

Figure 5.6: Incorrect holding position: instrument on right leg

While shorter players might be able to rest the instrument on the left leg when seated, most adults will need to either support the instrument's weight with the left arm, use a stand or pillow to raise the instrument to the needed height, or use a brace such as the ERGObrass system (see figure 5.4).

In no case should a top-valve euphonium be allowed to rest on the right leg (see figure 5.6), as this necessitates an unhelpful twisting of the torso in order to reach the mouthpiece. (In some instances this may be permissible with front-valve instruments.)

While there are products available which support the instrument in the standing position, in most cases you will need to support the instrument with your left arm. (see figure 5.7).

The Low Brass Player's Guide to Doubling

Figure 5.7: Correct standing position

Even if the instrument is resting on a stand, pillow, or your left leg, the left arm should be primarily responsible for providing balance. While the area between the right thumb and forefinger provides an additional balance point, supporting weight with the right thumb is inadvisable because the right arm, hand, and fingers must remain relaxed in order to facilitate quick finger motion.

The right fingers should be gently curved as though holding an aluminum beverage can—not flattened or curved sharply (see figures 5.8-10). The padded parts of the finger tips should rest on the center of the valve buttons; pressing on the sides of the valve buttons causes the valves to be depressed at a slight angle, slowing the rebound of the valves and causing permanent

Figure 5.8: Correct right hand position

Figure 5.9: Incorrect right hand position: excessive curve

Figure 5.10: Incorrect right hand position: flat fingers

damage over the long-term. For instruments with the fourth valve operated by the left hand, the curvature and operation of the left index finger should be similar to that of the right fingers. While complete elimination of the left arm's support function is impossible, the index finger at least should be allowed to remain relaxed.

Sound Concept

An uncharacteristic timbre is the most common error found among trombone to euphonium doublers. Even players relatively skilled with regard to fingering do not always make the necessary mental change from a trombone to a euphonium sound, and the resulting timbre is best described as that of a woofy valve trombone. The first step to develop a characteristic euphonium sound is to have the correct mental concept. Listening to great euphonium players certainly helps with this; I have also found it helpful to think of a tuba sound when playing the euphonium. After all, the euphonium is the tenor member of the tuba family, having a similarly conical bore and dark, warm sound—it is even called a tenor tuba in some contexts. Thinking of the euphonium as a tenor tuba eliminates the tendency to play with a bad trombone sound and promotes the creation of a uniform section sound with the tubas, with which the euphoniums are often paired in ensembles.

A characteristic euphonium timbre includes vibrato. While the use of vibrato has become an accepted part of both solo and ensemble playing on all brass instruments, it is practically required of euphonium players, possibly because of that instrument's deep association with British brass bands, a genre in which a pronounced vibrato is quite common. A lip/jaw vibrato (produced by thinking or saying "yah-yah-yah" while sustaining a note) is preferred over an airstream vibrato because the lip/jaw vibrato does not disrupt the flow of air through the instrument. The technique for producing this vibrato is essentially the same on the trombone and euphonium, so if you have already mastered it on trombone you should be able to do it on euphonium. If you have not yet learned to produce a lip/jaw vibrato, begin working on it immediately.

The Airstream

Perhaps the most important step for a trombonist to achieve a good euphonium sound is to modify the airstream. The tubing of the trombone is primarily cylindrical, maintaining a constant diameter through most of the instrument's length, and has few bends. The euphonium, conversely, is conical, with the tubing continually increasing in diameter and with a number of curves between mouthpiece and bell. On trombone, the cylindrical tubing and limited resistance require a direct and energetic way of blowing producing a brighter sound than on the euphonium, whose conical tubing, greater resistance (due to the curves in the tubing), and darker sound concept require a more expansive and somewhat more relaxed way of blowing. When playing the euphonium, think of blowing a stream of air that is warm, moist, relaxed, and continually expanding throughout and beyond the instrument—I sometimes advise students to imagine that the ceiling is a mirror which should be entirely fogged up as they play (this concept assumes an upward-pointing bell). By comparison, the airstream on the trombone is blown in a more compact and direct way, so it is directed toward a certain section of the opposite wall rather than the entire surface of that wall. The sound is still "big," but more focused. These visualizations for approaching euphonium blowing versus trombone blowing are mind tricks more than anything else. I have found they yield the desired results, though the actual difference between these two types of blowing, if precisely measured somehow, might be shown to be rather limited. The important thing is that this way of thinking *works*, and in a way that prevents you from becoming overly encumbered by thinking about small physical actions when playing.

Keep in mind, again, that such mind tricks will not be effective unless you have a correct concept of how the euphonium should sound. Remember that the euphonium is a tenor tuba and actively pursue that kind of sound. Listen to great players and emulate their sounds. Thinking of a warm, expansive, and relaxed airstream will not be effective unless it is directed toward achieving a desired timbre.

Intonation

Skilled trombonists are accustomed to making needed intonation adjustments using the handslide, a convenience that is not available on the euphonium. Happily, there are several methods of adjusting pitch that are available to the euphonium player, and in some cases these can be used in combination to achieve the desired result.

Playing in tune demands that the instrument's tuning slides be adjusted using a tuner or other reference before beginning. The simplicity of the trombone's one, two, or three tuning slides stands in sharp contrast to the euphonium; four-valve compensating instruments have *seven* tuning slides, and finding the best placement for these slides is a prerequisite for playing in tune (see figure 5.11). I recommend placing the main tuning slide so B-flat is in tune, the second valve slide placed so A is in

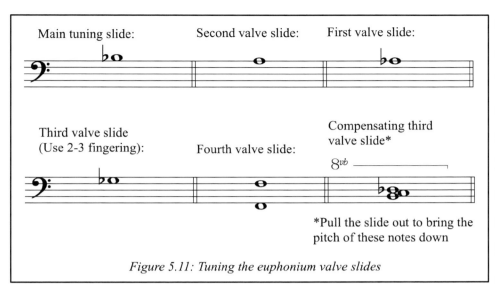

Figure 5.11: Tuning the euphonium valve slides

tune, and the first valve slide so A-flat is in tune. The third valve slide should be placed so G-flat is in tune using the 2-3 fingering combination, as tuning the third valve alone will leave the 2-3 combination sharp. This tuning makes the third valve alone yield a slightly flat version of the 1-2 combination, a sometimes useful alternate fingering. To place the fourth valve slide, check both middle and low F; if these do not agree choose the placement for the lower note as long as this does not make C in the staff depart too much from its usual slightly sharp tendency. The compensating tubing, when present, includes short but moveable tuning slides on the first and third valves. The first is too short to be useful for tuning purposes, but the third can be adjusted a bit. I usually extend that slide slightly to lower the pitch of D-flat, C, and B. Already you see that tuning a valved instrument is an exercise in compromise, and very much an art rather than a science. However, if the best tuning placement is not found, the adjustments needed during practice and performance will be even greater and sometimes impossibly difficult.

The simplest means of adjusting pitch on the euphonium while playing is bending or lipping the pitch by slightly tightening or loosening the embouchure muscles. Lipping is not recommended on trombone because it leads to a poor tone quality, and is unnecessary in any case. The euphonium, however, is more forgiving of such adjustments than the trombone; one can sometimes bend the pitch a quarter-step or more in either direction with little decline in tone quality. This is enough to correct a large number of intonation problems, and in the middle and lower registers often occurs unconsciously, even with young and inexperienced players. Lipping pitches in the upper register is more difficult and does not always yield the same tone quality as doing so elsewhere in the range. In the upper register—or whenever lipping pitches proves to be ineffective—the use of alternate fingerings might prove to be a more effective means of adjusting pitch.

Every brass player should be thoroughly familiar with the overtone series for each fingering on every instrument played. This is the easiest way to have not only a thorough knowledge of all of the fingering possibilities for a given note, but also an equally thorough knowledge of the intonation tendencies of each of those fingerings. This is simpler than it may sound at first; every partial in the overtone series has a certain tuning tendency, and these tendencies are the same on every brass instrument. For example, the fifth partial tends to be slightly flat on all brass instruments, the sixth slightly sharp, and the seventh so flat that it is unusable (except on the trombone, where a substantial handslide adjustment can be made). While certain notes will deviate from this norm on each individual instrument, the normal tuning tendencies of each partial will hold true in the vast majority of cases. The player who knows the overtone series well can readily choose fingerings to adjust intonation as needed. If, for example, D above the staff is flat when played open in the fifth partial and the player is unable to adequately bend the pitch up with the embouchure, the 1-2 alternate fingering might solve the problem; this puts the note in the sixth partial and might actually sound a little sharp as a result, meaning the player may have to lip the note down to be in tune. A third option is to play the D with the third valve.

The thought process described above might appear cumbersome and impractical in written form, but in practice it takes place almost instantaneously and even subconsciously in the mind of an experienced player. Strive to attain a complete and thorough knowledge of the overtone chart for the euphonium and every other instrument you play, including both the notes and the tuning tendencies for each partial. By doing so you will give yourself the largest number of fingering possibilities for each note, with accompanying improvements in both intonation and technical facility.

While lipping pitches and choosing alternate fingerings are the primary means of correcting intonation problems on euphonium, there are some limited possibilities for correcting pitch by altering the length of the instrument. The simplest of these is a trigger mechanism attached to the main tuning slide (see figure 5.12); the most common mechanism is a metal linkage

Figure 5.12: Main tuning slide trigger

that attaches to the tuning slide on one end and to a paddle operated by the left thumb on the other. When the paddle is depressed the tuning slide extends, lowering the pitch. The length of extension is determined by how far the player depresses the paddle, but the adjustment is fairly subtle, with the tuning slide moving a little over an inch at most. While these trigger mechanisms are an effective means of correcting sharp pitches, they offer no means of raising flat ones. Additionally, they add weight to the instrument, a negative aspect which for some players outweighs (pun intended) the benefit of pitch correction.

While compensating euphoniums are the norm among professional players (at least those for whom euphonium is a primary instrument), these instruments are no panacea regarding low register intonation. This design gives the euphonium a fully chromatic lower register and improved intonation when using valve combinations including the fourth valve, but certain notes still sound somewhat sharp or flat and must be adjusted. The compensating system *improves* low-register intonation; it does not *perfect* it.

Articulation

Slurred passages are executed on the euphonium by blowing a steady stream of air while moving the valves in a relaxed manner. The biggest mistake you can make when slurring on euphonium is to think of it as simply the absence of tonguing. While slurs are normally executed without the tongue, if slurring technique is to be effective it must be defined positively, in terms of what one *does* in order to slur, rather than only negatively, in terms of what one *does not* do. Slurring is a type of legato, and just as legato tonguing on the trombone (and every other wind instrument) requires a steady airstream, so does slurring on the euphonium (and, again, every other wind instrument). Additionally, the valve action should be *slightly* more relaxed when slurring than when tonguing. This might be counterintuitive to trombonists, who are usually accustomed to moving the slide rapidly in legato passages to avoid unwanted glissandi. Nevertheless, depressing the valves in a hard or abrupt manner can create a slight articulation which disrupts the sound of effective slurring. Changes in vowel shape can be employed as needed when large melodic leaps occur in slurred passages, just as when playing lip-slur exercises.

As long as you blow a steady airstream when doing so, slurring on the euphonium is usually easy to master. Tongued articulations, however, can be a bit trickier. You must tongue somewhat harder to produce a given articulation on the euphonium than to produce the same articulation on trombone.

For whatever reason, tonguing in precisely the same way on the euphonium as on the trombone yields an articulation that lacks crispness and definition, so increase the hardness of tongued articulations until the desired sound is achieved. Multiple-tonguing especially must be executed with more vigor. While the directive to tongue harder is simple enough, it does feel odd at first. Just remember that you must play using the method that yields the right *sound*, regardless of how it *feels*.

Clefs and Transposition

When music for euphonium is written in bass clef it is normally in concert pitch (i.e. the written and sounding pitches are identical), but when music for the euphonium is written in treble clef, the euphonium is treated as a transposing instrument with the sounding pitch a major ninth lower than the written pitch. Reading transposing treble clef parts is a skill that must be mastered, as they are frequently used in all types of music for the euphonium and a concert pitch bass clef part is not always available.

Figure 5.13: Reading treble clef euphonium parts using tenor clef

When reading a treble clef euphonium part, trombonists can imagine the part is in tenor clef in concert pitch and add two flats to (or subtract two sharps from) the key signature (see figure 5.13). This system allows one to read treble clef euphonium parts without transposing with the following exceptions: written C-sharp becomes B-natural in tenor clef; written F-natural becomes E-flat in tenor clef; and written F-sharp becomes E-natural in tenor clef.

As an added bonus, learning this little trick will also enable you to read the transposing trombone parts in treble clef that appear in some contexts, such as in British brass band music.

Written parts for euphonium which use tenor and alto clefs in concert pitch are rare, though tenor clef does appear from time to time. Alto clef is practically never used, except as a trick for reading an extremely unusual transposition: that of the "tenor tuba in B-flat" parts which appear in the orchestral tenor tuba parts of Richard Strauss and perhaps others. The music for these parts is written

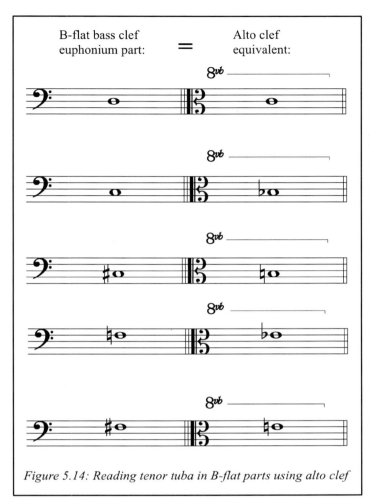

Figure 5.14: Reading tenor tuba in B-flat parts using alto clef

in bass clef, but the sounding pitch is a whole step lower than written. This is a rarely-encountered way of writing for the euphonium and in most cases concert pitch parts have been made available for works which use it, but if you find yourself having to read one of these parts there are two methods that can be used: transpose at sight, reading every written note a whole-step lower; or read the part in alto clef down an octave (see figure 5.14), while adding two flats or subtracting two sharps from the key signature. Fortunately this transposition is rarely used; learning to read transposing treble clef parts will take care of the majority of the demands for transposition encountered when playing the euphonium.

Mutes

Mutes are called for much less frequently in euphonium parts than in trombone parts, but a euphonium straight mute might be a wise purchase for a trombone/euphonium doubler, particularly if you plan to perform a good deal of solo and chamber music. Select a mute which fits into your instrument well and provides a good sound and consistent intonation, keeping in mind that you will need to pull the main tuning slide a bit to compensate for the sharpness caused by the mute. You may need to change or adjust the corks, as well. It is best to delay purchasing a mute until after purchasing an instrument, as finding a good match between mute and instrument can sometimes be tricky.

Euphonium Versus Baritone Horn

The euphonium and baritone horn share the same fundamental pitch, tonal range, and fingerings. Both instruments are available with three or four valves, and even with compensating systems.

Players of either instrument could pick up the other and immediately play competently without additional training (though not always with a refined characteristic sound), even reading the same written music. The similarities between the two instruments are thus significant and account in part for the confusion between the two. The differences between the two instruments are in bore size, bore profile, bell diameter, and mouthpiece size. While the euphonium has a larger bore, primarily conical tubing, a fairly large bell, and a deep mouthpiece, the baritone horn has a smaller bore and primarily cylindrical tubing, a smaller bell (usually the diameter of a large-bore tenor trombone or smaller bass trombone bell), and a smaller and shallower mouthpiece, not unlike one that might be used on a small-bore tenor trombone (see figure 5.15). These smaller dimensions make the baritone horn shorter and narrower (in terms of appearance and handling, not tubing length) than the euphonium with a correspondingly smaller and brighter sound—one that can be described as more trombone-like than that of the more tuba-like euphonium.

Figure 5.15: Baritone horn

The baritone horn is rarely used in the United States. The genre in which it is most commonly used is the brass bands prevalent in Great Britain and elsewhere in Europe, and which are slowly beginning to proliferate in North America. In these ensembles the baritone horns and euphoniums constitute two separate sections, playing different parts and with their distinct timbres used to great effect.

With British-style brass bands becoming more common in North America, the possibility of wanting to double on baritone horn is becoming greater. Learning fingerings is the same as for the euphonium, but the approach to blowing and timbre should be more akin to that used on the trombone. For the trombonist, this means that the leap to doubling on baritone horn will be even shorter than to doubling on the euphonium. Of course, as with any instrument, having a proper sound concept is a vital part of achieving success. Listening to fine players on the baritone horn and using

The Low Brass Player's Guide to Doubling

them as models is thus of paramount importance for the baritone horn doubler.

Suggested Practice and Performance Literature

These solo repertoire suggestions are almost evenly divided between original works and transcriptions, but all take particular advantage of the euphonium's strengths and should be accessible to newer doublers. Among the method books, the Mead volumes particularly promote the cultivation of a characteristic euphonium timbre in distinction from a trombone one; the Bordogni etudes can be effectively employed for this purpose, as well. The Vining book, like the comparable volumes for tenor and bass trombones, promotes correct use of the body when breathing and playing. The Payne collection of band and orchestral excerpts furthers this goal, in addition to providing exposure to common performance and audition materials. The Arnold, Brahms, and Fink books will strengthen your ability to execute parts written in a transposing treble clef, while Arban and Kopprasch, along with the prescribed fundamental exercises and scale and arpeggio studies, aid the development of greater technical facility.

Method Books

Arban, Jean-Baptiste, edited by Joseph Alessi and Dr. Brian Bowman - *Complete Method for Trombone and Euphonium*

Arnold, Jay (compiler) - *Masterworks for Trumpet*

Bordogni, Giulio Marco, annotated and edited by Michael Mulcahy - *Complete Vocalises for Trombone*

Brahms, Johannes, edited by EF Goldman - *12 Etudes for Trumpet*

Clarke, Herbert. L., edited by Claude Gordon - *Technical Studies for Bass Clef Instruments*

Concone, Giuseppe, transcribed and edited by John Korak - *The Complete Solfeggi*

Fink, Reginald H. - *Introducing the Tenor Clef for Trombone*

Horowitz, Michael, compiler - *The Real Book*

Kopprasch, Georg, edited by Keith Brown - *60 Studies for Trombone* (2 vols.)

Mead, Steven (ed.) - *New Concert Studies* (2 vols.)

Payne, Barbara (compiler), edited by Brian Bowman and David R. Werden - *Euphonium Excerpts from the Standard Band and Orchestra Library*

Remington, Emory, edited by Donald Hunsberger - *The Remington Warm-Up Studies*

The Low Brass Player's Guide to Doubling

Schlossberg, Max, edited by C.K. Schlossberg - *Daily Drills and Technical Studies for Trombone*

Vining, David - *The Breathing Book for Euphonium*

Solo Repertoire

Capuzzi, Antonio, arranged and adapted by Philip Catelinet - *Andante and Rondo* from *Concerto for Double Bass*

Curnow, James - *Rhapsody for Euphonium*

De Luca, Joseph - *Beautiful Colorado*

Falcone, Nicholas D. - *Mazurka for Solo Euphonium*

Richards, Goff - *Midnight Euphonium*

Sparke, Philip - *Aubade*

Telemann, Georg Philipp, edited by Allen Ostrander and Robert Veyron-Lecroix - *Sonata in F Minor*

Schumann, Robert, arranged by Paul Droste - *Five Pieces in Folk Style, op. 102*

Vaughan Williams, Ralph - *Six Studies in English Folksong*

White, Donald H. - *Lyric Suite for Euphonium and Piano*

Appendix E: Euphonium and Baritone Horn Resources

Targeted Fundamentals 153

Fingering Chart 156

Overtone Series Chart 158

Chapter 6: Trombonists Doubling on Tuba

Frank Gazda

As with any other double, finding an appropriate instrument and mouthpiece, learning mechanics, cultivating a characteristic sound, and developing a practice methodology are critical for successful tuba doubling. This chapter covers strategies for achieving these goals; you may wish to consult the previous chapter on trombone/euphonium doubling, as many of the concepts presented there will also apply to doubling on tuba.

Choosing an Instrument

When choosing and purchasing a tuba you must consider three primary characteristics of the instrument: key, type of valves, and size. These variables are interrelated and have a significant effect on the playing characteristics of the instrument.

Key

The key of the tuba refers to the fundamental pitch of the open instrument, with no valves pressed down. There are four standard keys of tuba: F, E-flat, B-flat (referred to as BB-flat), and C (referred to as CC). Each key of tuba has a different length of tubing and a corresponding different set of fingerings. Any key of instrument can be used in any situation, but some keys will be better suited to a given situation than others.

Tubas are categorized as bass tubas in F or E-flat and contrabass tubas in CC or BB-flat. Bass tubas are shorter and consequently favor the upper register, typically have lighter sounds, and are preferred for solo repertoire, chamber music, and higher orchestral parts. Contrabass tubas are longer, tend to favor the lower register, and are usually best in larger ensemble settings. Full-time professional tuba players usually own and play more than one key of instrument to adequately cover all situations.

The F tuba has the shortest length and highest pitch of the standard tubas. Its fundamental pitch is a perfect fourth below that of the tenor and bass trombones; because of this it has the quickest response and easiest accuracy in the middle and upper registers of all the tubas. However, the F tuba has a smaller sound, often with less breadth in the lower register. Old F tubas can have a stuffy low range, but this problem has been solved with more recent models. A fifth valve is a must for the F tuba, especially if it is to be your only tuba, and a sixth valve may be advisable, as these additional valves are expressly designed to correct intonation problems, which will be discussed in greater detail shortly. If your work as a tuba doubler is going to be mainly as a soloist and in smaller ensembles, the F tuba could be a good choice, but if you anticipate playing in a larger ensemble or spending more time in the low register, this will not be the best choice for you.

The E-flat tuba is pitched one step lower than the F tuba. It shares the F tuba's easy response and accuracy in the middle and upper registers, but has a broader sound than the F tuba and is therefore stronger in the low range. Modern E-flat tubas are equipped with either a fifth valve or a compensating system to improve low register intonation. As mentioned in the previous chapter, the compensating system adds additional tubing when the fourth valve is engaged, improving the intonation so a fifth valve is not needed. However, the low register on compensating E-flat tubas can be stuffy, and the compensating system adds weight. Still, a compensating E-flat tuba with a 19-inch bell has been the preferred all-around tuba in the United Kingdom for years and is a very versatile instrument.

The CC tuba is the preferred contrabass tuba of most classical tubists in the United States. It has the weighty sound of a bigger instrument but easier response and better clarity than a BB-flat tuba. Some have suggested that the CC tuba is popular in orchestras because the fingerings are easier in sharp keys than on a BB-flat. In any case, for many performers the CC tuba provides the desired mix of clarity and breadth. A four-valve CC tuba is adequate for most uses, although a fifth valve is very useful for adjusting intonation, particularly in the lower register.

The BB-flat tuba is the main contrabass tuba in Germany, as well as among student tubists in the United States. A good BB-flat has a depth of sound in the low register that tubas in other keys cannot match. For the doubler, the main disadvantage of a BB-flat tuba is difficulty in achieving clear articulation and accurate pitches in the middle and upper registers. For a trombonist, the fingerings on a BB-flat tuba are relatively easy to learn because it is pitched exactly one octave lower than the tenor and bass trombones, and the fingerings are easy to associate to slide positions. If you also play euphonium, the fingerings on the BB-flat tuba are identical to the euphonium, but an octave lower. A four-valve BB-flat tuba is adequate for most uses; five-valve BB-flats are uncommon, and BB-flat tubas with compensating systems are used in British brass bands but are rare outside of that context, largely due to their excessive weight.

Figure 6.1: German style BB-flat tuba with rotary valves - Miraphone 187 (left); American style F tuba with piston valves - Yamaha YFB-621 (right)

Rotary Valves Versus Piston Valves

The choice of valve type is a subject of great debate in the tuba community, and must also factor into your choice of instrument. The difference is not only in the type of valves but also in the overall design of the tuba, creating a noticeable difference in sound characteristics.

Rotary valve tubas usually have larger bores and more resistance than piston valve tubas, though this is somewhat mitigated by the taper of the instrument. Rotary valve tubas have longer leadpipes than most piston valve tubas; thus, the expansion of the bore into the conical taper starts later in the length of tubing, resulting in a more funnel-shaped bell. This generally provides a more centered column of sound. Tubas with this design are sometimes generically referred to as "German Style" tubas (see figure 6.1).

The Low Brass Player's Guide to Doubling

Piston valve tubas typically have shorter leadpipes, allowing for earlier expansion of the tubing from mouthpiece to bell, larger top and bottom bows, a wider taper in the bell, and frequently a larger bell diameter. This can result in a wider, more organ-like quality to the sound with less clarity. These tubas are sometimes called "American Style" tubas.

Size

Size should not be confused with the key of the instrument. The key is dependent on the length of the tubing, while size refers to the dimensions of the bore, bell, and the taper of the tubing. It is possible to have varying sizes of tubas in the same or different keys. Tubas are generally referred to as 3/4, 4/4, 5/4, and 6/4, and these size references are fairly standard across the industry (although some manufacturers' size descriptions vary from the consensus). A 4/4 tuba is standard or full size and will suffice for the majority of the doubler's needs. A 3/4 tuba (slightly smaller in the aforementioned dimensions) may be better for chamber music, pit orchestras, and solos, while a 5/4 or 6/4 instrument is best suited for large ensembles.

Making Your Choice

When choosing your instrument, you must take all of these factors into account. While full-time tubists improve their versatility by playing two or more instruments, economic considerations usually dictate that doublers have only one. The type of music you plan to play will influence the key and size of your instrument. Many outstanding tubists play both piston and rotary instruments, so that choice is typically determined by personal preference for sound, playing characteristics, and ergonomics. Bear in mind that combining the variables of key and size in different ways can yield some surprising results; for example, a 6/4 F tuba may have a bigger sound than a 3/4 CC tuba.

It is critical that you test a few different tubas before choosing. Many doublers choose an E-flat tuba, while others choose a 4/4 or 3/4 BB-flat or CC tuba—all very versatile choices that have strong advantages for a doubler. Occasionally a music director or conductor will express a preference for a particular key or type of instrument, though in most cases the tuba doubler should simply choose the instrument that does the greatest number of things well.

A Note on the Sousaphone

If you find yourself playing traditional jazz you might explore purchasing a sousaphone rather

The Low Brass Player's Guide to Doubling

than a concert tuba. Most sousaphones are in the key of BB-flat, with a few in the key of E-flat. Most have three valves, although a few makers produce four-valve sousaphones. Fiberglass sousaphones are less expensive and are considerably lighter, but most tubists agree that brass sousaphones have a superior sound.

Choosing a Mouthpiece

A poor mouthpiece choice can have a negative effect on response and intonation on tuba. There are dozens of mouthpiece manufacturers, but a certain lack of standardization in the sizing and labeling of tuba mouthpieces complicates comparing the mouthpieces from different manufacturers using catalog descriptions alone. Visiting a music store with several choices or a tuba conference where many dealers will have displays is the best way to find the right mouthpiece for you and your instrument. With that in mind, the following are general considerations.

The shank must match the mouthpiece receiver. Most modern tubas take either an American or European shank mouthpiece—these are close in size and most tubas will accept either. Some older tubas (especially British E-flat tubas) take a small shank (about the same size as a large shank trombone mouthpiece), while some larger tubas may take a larger shank mouthpiece (usually designated L or XL by the mouthpiece makers).

A broad generalization is that mouthpieces with bowl-shaped cups work best with rotary valve tubas and funnel-shaped cups work best with piston valve tubas. Again, trying a variety of mouthpieces with your instrument is critical.

Unsurprisingly, trombonists usually find that a relatively small tuba mouthpiece works best for them, as mouthpieces that are too large can lead to difficulties with accuracy and articulation. Mouthpieces with cup diameters of 32-32.5 mm will provide a good departure point for mouthpiece experimentation. Common models in this size range include the Schilke 66, Bach 24AW, Bach 18, and Conn Helleberg 7B. A mouthpiece such as the Bach 24AW, which combines a narrow diameter with a deep cup, can be an effective choice for a trombone/tuba doubler.

Mutes

In recent years, tuba mutes have become increasingly common, especially in solo and chamber music. While it is still possible to go an entire doubling career and never need one, if you plan to double frequently it is best to be prepared. The most important thing to remember when choosing a mute is that the mute must fit your tuba. With so much diversity in bell size and taper among tubas, you most assuredly need to wait until you purchase your own instrument before finding a mute to match, especially given the high price tag of tuba mutes.

Just like trombone mutes, tuba mutes can make your pitch sharp and can be stuffy in the low register. You can adjust the fit and resistance of the mute by adding or shaving the corks. An old trick is to lengthen the mute by putting a cylinder made of a rolled up piece of paper (stiffer, like card stock is best) in the end of the mute. This can bring the pitch down and help low register response, but it can also eliminate some of the muted timbre.

Holding Position

Figure 6.2: Correct tuba holding position

As with all brass instruments, having correct posture is necessary to play the tuba in a relaxed, tension- free manner (see figure 6.2). Not only will this help your breathing, but poor posture can be uncomfortable and even lead to long-term pain and stress-related injuries. You should sit up straight and relaxed, bringing the mouthpiece to you rather than raising or lowering your head to meet the mouthpiece (see figure 6.3). It is very important that the tuba fit you physically. You must be able to reach all valves comfortably, and your left arm must be able to reach the valve tuning slides and balance the instrument. The optimum finger position for both rotary and piston valves is with the

The Low Brass Player's Guide to Doubling

Figure 6.3: Incorrect tuba holding positions
Mouthpiece too high (left) and mouthpiece too low (right)

fingers slightly curved and centered exactly on the valve button or valve paddle (see figure 6.4). This position ensures all the finger motion is straight down and is more efficient than wasting motion by pushing at an angle. Keeping the fingers straight and flat causes technical difficulties (especially with piston valves) by slowing down the rebound of the

Figure 6.4: Correct right hand position

58

The Low Brass Player's Guide to Doubling

Figure 6.5: Incorrect right hand positions excessive arch (left) and flat fingers (right)

valves, and may also cause the valves to wear unevenly over time (see figure 6.5). The photos in this section illustrate correct and incorrect finger positions on a rotary valve tuba; refer to the similar photos in the previous chapter for guidance regarding piston instruments.

Common Ergonomic Problems and Solutions

PROBLEM: The tuba is too tall, forcing the player to stretch to reach the mouthpiece.
SOLUTION: Use a tuba stand (see figure 6.6); a tripod that sits in front of the chair with a u-shaped cup to hold the tuba. Many players choose to use tuba stands even if height is not a

Figure 6.6: Tuba stand

problem, as they offer more consistency when using different chairs and can be more comfortable. Popular stands are made by K & M and Baltimore Brass, among others.

PROBLEM: The tuba is too short, forcing the player to hunch over.

SOLUTION: Make a homemade "tuba block" out of wood or other materials. I have used old papers cut to a 4 x 6 inch rectangle, stacked to the proper height and then wrapped in duct tape, to raise my tuba from my chair. The aforementioned tuba stands can also help with this issue.

PROBLEM: The valve buttons are too far apart to comfortably reach (more common with piston than rotary tubas).

SOLUTION: This is not an easily solved issue, and is an important reason to test a tuba prior to purchasing it. If the valves on a tuba are not comfortably placed, you may need to look for a different model. Changing the angle of your hand to the valves may help, if your arms are long enough.

PROBLEM: The thumb ring is in an uncomfortable position.

SOLUTION: Some thumb rings are adjustable and can be turned to different angles. Many players simply choose to have the thumb ring removed—an easy modification for any repair technician.

PROBLEM: The leadpipe is too short and the player cannot get the tuba close enough to the body.

SOLUTION: Angle the instrument, rotating the mouthpiece closer to you. If this does not work, a good repair technician can change the height and angle of the leadpipe, but an easier solution is to purchase a different model.

Fingerings

Many trombone players initially learn tuba or euphonium fingerings by matching slide positions with the equivalent fingering. This only works with the BB-flat tuba, and with an octave displacement. The fourth valve lowers the pitch of the instrument a perfect fourth, and can thus be thought of as equivalent to the F-attachment on trombone. The fifth valve, when present, will typically be tuned to a flat whole step (about halfway between third and fourth positions) and is used to bring some of the sharp low notes into tune.

The Low Brass Player's Guide to Doubling

Tenor Trombone with F Attachment Slide Positions	Bass Trombone (F/G-flat/D) Slide Positions	Non-Compensating BB-flat Tuba Fingerings (four valves)	Non-Compensating BB-flat Tuba Fingerings (five valves)
1	1	Open	Open
2	2	2	2
3	3	1	1
4	4	1-2, or 3	1-2, or 3
5	5, or Gb1	2-3	2-3
6, or F1	6, F1, or Gb2	4, or 1-3	4, or 1-3
7, or F2	7, F2, or Gb3	2-4, or 1-2-3	2-4, or 1-2-3
F3	F3, or Gb4	1-4, or 1-2-4	1-4, 1-2-4, or 4-5
F4	F4, Gb5, or D1	2-3-4	2-3-4
F5	F5, Gb6, or D2	1-3-4	1-3-4, or 3-4-5
F6	F6, or D3	1-2-3-4	1-2-3-4, 2-3-4-5, or 1-3-4-5
Not Present	D4	Not Present	1-2-3-4-5

Tubas other than the BB-flat lack such direct comparisons to the trombone (except E-flat tuba to the alto trombone), but the general principle holds that the second valve lowers the pitch by a half-step, the first valve a whole-step, the combined first and second valves (or the third valve) a minor third, the combined second and third valves a major third, the fourth valve a perfect fourth, etc. Once this principle is understood, learning the fingerings for any tuba becomes relatively easy, especially if you have a thorough knowledge of the overtone series for your instrument. Overtone series charts for all the tubas appear in Appendix F.

All bass clef tuba parts are in concert pitch, regardless of the instrument played. Therefore, different keyed tubas have different fingerings. Players who treat different keyed tubas as transposing instruments are rare; the music does not transpose so neither should you. The need to learn multiple sets of fingerings is simply an attendant difficulty of tuba playing.

The best way to develop valve facility is to practice lots of scales and drills. I suggest reading the scales extensively before playing them from memory, as you need to develop the ability to see a written pitch and match it with the correct fingering, in addition to developing speed and reflexes on regular fingering patterns. There are several technical studies books listed at the end of this chapter which are suitable for this need. Two patterns I find to be extremely helpful are revolving scale patterns and scales in thirds, both of which are part of the scale and arpeggio routine which appears in Appendix B.

Clefs and Transposition

The vast majority of tuba music is written in bass clef in concert pitch, but a notable exception to this rule is the tuba parts in British-style brass bands. Such ensembles have enjoyed a great surge in popularity in the United States in recent years, and you may have the opportunity to join one. Traditional British-style brass bands have two E-flat tubas and two BB-flat tubas. Depending on the band, tubas in any key may be welcome, but the music for the two tuba parts will be notated in E-flat treble clef and B-flat treble

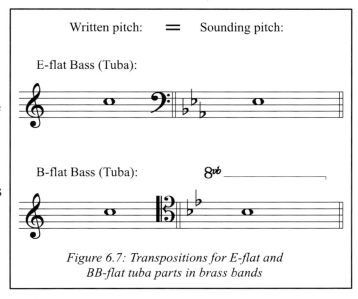

Figure 6.7: Transpositions for E-flat and BB-flat tuba parts in brass bands

clef. The E-flat transposition is straightforward: pretend the music is in bass clef and add three flats. The B-flat transposition is trickier—it is similar to the transposition for treble clef euphonium parts, but with an additional octave displacement. You can read B-flat tuba parts in brass bands as tenor clef, down an octave, with two added flats (see figure 6.7). Of course, you can always choose to forego these transposition shortcuts and simply learn to read and think in transposed pitch.

Sound Concept

The tuba sound is characteristically darker, broader, and somewhat less direct than the trombone sound, but it is important to find a good balance between a big sound and a focused sound. Aim too much for a large sound and you may develop an unfocused, tubby sound, yet going too far in the other direction can result in a tight, pinched tone quality. A good general tuba sound will have enough core to provide a clear pitch and enough breadth to support the ensemble. Playing in ensembles with good tubists and listening to recordings of the world's top players will help you develop and refine your tuba sound.

The Airstream

When switching from trombone to tuba you must play with a larger, more relaxed airstream. In other words, move a larger volume of air under less air pressure. Thinking of blowing an expansive

The Low Brass Player's Guide to Doubling

stream of air freely through the tuba's constantly expanding conical tubing can also help. Breathing exercises are very important for tubists, whether the tuba is one's primary or secondary instrument. A very helpful exercise is to get a pinwheel and simply inhale for one beat and exhale for one beat, spinning the pinwheel in a fast but relaxed fashion.

The Embouchure

Like the airstream, a good tuba embouchure may feel more relaxed than a trombone embouchure. While no two embouchures are the same, it is important to maintain firmness in your corners and a flat chin, even on tuba. Some puffing of the cheeks in the low register is not unusual, but monitor this for adverse effects to your sound or control.

Sometimes trombonists attempt to play tuba with a trombone embouchure. This will lead to splitting notes, difficulties getting a full sound, and problems playing in the low register. When buzzing the tuba mouthpiece, make sure the entire lip surface within the mouthpiece is vibrating. Experiment with different embouchure settings and air volumes until you are getting a full "tuba buzz." If you have difficulties buzzing in the low register on the mouthpiece alone, plugging the mouthpiece into a six to eight inch length of rubber tubing can provide enough resistance to help. Buzzing your mouthpiece into the pinwheel mentioned above will give you a good idea of the volume of air needed.

Intonation

A trombonist with a good ear may simply adjust the handslide without really thinking about the tendencies of the instrument, but understanding the intonation tendencies of the tuba is critical to solving intonation issues on that instrument.

Tuning Slide Placement

Playing in tune requires that each tuning slide be placed in an optimum default position, although slides that are reachable can be manually adjusted in order to correct particular notes as needed. As was recommended for the euphonium in the previous chapter, the main tuning slide should be placed so that the octaves of the open fundamental are in tune, and that those for the first, second, and fourth valves should be placed so that the octaves of the fundamental pitches for each of those valves

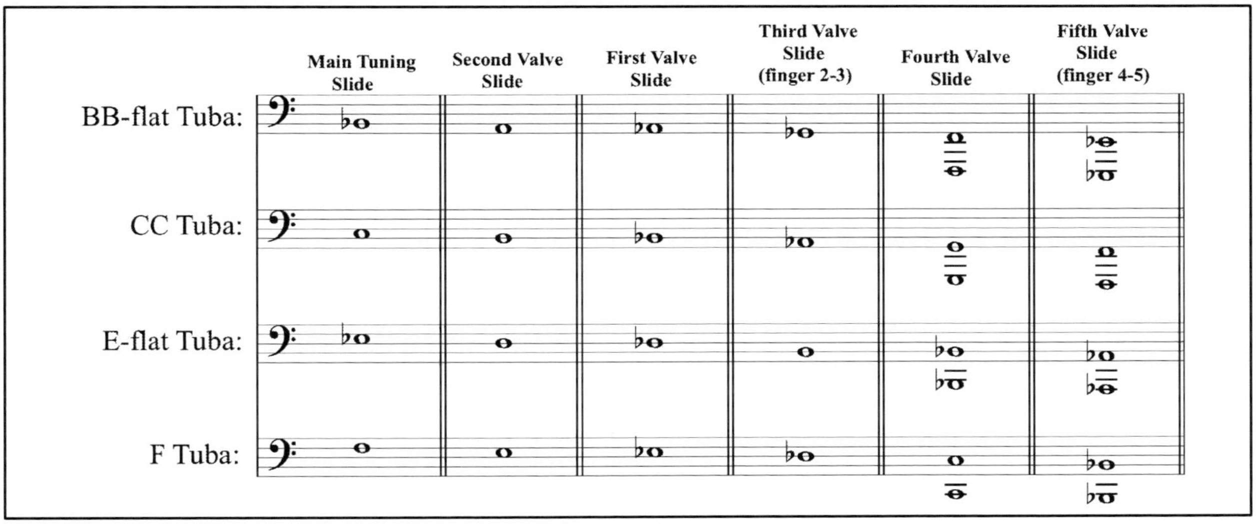

Figure 6.8: Tuba valve slide tuning

independently are in tune. The third valve slide should be placed so that the octaves of the fundamental for the 2-3 combination are in tune, understanding that this will cause pitches using the third valve individually to be a bit flat. The fifth valve alone yields a flat whole step on most instruments. I recommend placing it so that the octaves of the fundamental using the 4-5 combination are in tune, though you might choose to place that slide to tune a different combination at your discretion (see figure 6.8).

Tuning Tendencies

The basic tuning tendencies of each partial of the overtone series are the same on every brass instrument. If you know the partial in which a given note lies for the fingering you are using, you will be able to anticipate its likely tuning tendency. It is therefore critical that you have a thorough knowledge of the overtone series for your instrument.

The more valves you engage, the lower the note but the sharper the relative pitch. First valve alone is more in tune than one and two together. One and three is decidedly sharp, and one, two, and three extremely sharp. Whenever you use valves in combination, expect to make adjustments to lower the pitch using the lips, by manipulating a tuning slide, or both.

Solving Intonation Problems

Minor pitch discrepancies can be solved by bending or lipping the notes into tune; however, extensive lipping is not recommended, as it will compromise tone quality and lead to embouchure fatigue. Additionally, some of the valve slides on the tuba can be moved to correct out of tune notes. The slides on most tubas are arranged so the performer has easy access to the first, third, and often fourth valve slides. When kept clean and well lubricated, these are easy to move while playing. When a note is too out of tune to easily adjust by slide pulling or lipping, alternate fingerings can be used. Some players prefer to use alternate fingerings instead of constantly pulling slides.

The addition of fourth, fifth, and sixth valves can solve some intonation problems. Just like the F-attachment on trombone, the fourth valve fills in most of the chromatic gap between the first and second partials and provides more in tune fingerings for certain valve combinations. The fifth valve fills in the missing notes the fourth valve cannot, and provides other options for tuning the low register. Some tubas even have a sixth valve, which can provide even more options.

It is very important that you spend a lot of time with a tuner and/or using tuning drones to learn what your tuba's tendencies are, and to decide exactly how you are going to compensate for them. A combination of the above techniques will likely be needed to achieve the best result.

Articulation

Getting a solid front to notes on the tuba can be tricky for players accustomed to smaller equipment. Buzzing the mouthpiece is a critical tool for developing clarity, and blowing on a pinwheel can help with getting immediate air at the front of the note.

It may seem somewhat counterintuitive, but using less tongue will often lead to clearer attacks, particularly in the lower register. Just as with any brass instrument, the trick is to get the embouchure buzzing immediately. The more immediate your air, the more immediate the tone. While the tongue is an important enunciator, the start of the note is caused by the air activating the buzz, and the tongue merely provides shape and definition to the beginning of the note. Over-tonguing blocks the air and can cause late or rough attacks. As a practice tool, I have found breath attacks one of the best ways to develop reliable articulation.

When single-tonguing fast notes on tuba, the tongue should remain fairly low in your mouth and stay relatively flat. To cultivate a reliable, appropriate articulation style, start by practicing rapid tonguing on a single note, then moving into five note scales and patterns.

Developing slurring is vitally important for the trombone/tuba doubler. Unlike the trombone, where some notes need to be legato tongued, this is rarely necessary on the tuba. Keep the air moving in a solid, relaxed stream with no dips or breaks in the airflow, keep your buzz constant, and

The Low Brass Player's Guide to Doubling

let the valves do the work. Try moving the valves very slowly, making sure that the break is filled in with buzz.

There are two schools of thought on legato valve technique: move the valves slowly to get more connection between the notes, or move the valves very quickly, eliminating space between the pitches. The challenge inherent in the first way is to make the buzz constant to fill the gaps between notes. If you choose to move the valves very quickly, be careful not to bump the airstream; fast-moving valves still need to have a smooth, even, relaxed airflow. Practice the fingering exercises in the targeted fundamentals with both techniques and see which is most comfortable for you.

Accuracy

One of the challenges of playing tuba is accuracy in the middle and upper registers. Because the BB-flat tuba is pitched one octave lower than the trombone, the pitches in the harmonic series that appear in the staff and above are closer together than on trombone because they are higher in the harmonic series. This can create a sort of accuracy illusion to a trombonist that potentially causes confusion as to which partial must be played. This problem is mitigated somewhat on the shorter tubas, but accuracy can still be a challenge for those accustomed to notes in the staff lying lower in the overtone series. Buzzing the mouthpiece, interval and harmonic series exercises, lip slurs, and singing problem passages are good ways to work on accuracy.

Suggested Practice and Performance Literature

The following method books and solos are part of the core of the tuba repertoire. The Arban book likely needs no explanation. This edition has been prepared with the CC tuba in mind, but it can be used with any tuba. The Bordogni *Vocalises* are the same as those appearing in editions for tenor trombone by Joannes Rochut and Michael Mulcahy. The Jacobs and Snedecor low register books are critical not only for developing the breadth of sound and breath control the tubist needs, but also for learning to read the notes four and five ledger lines below the staff that you will encounter. The Tyrell and Blazhevich books cover a fairly wide range and are good for working on the upper register as well as the middle and low registers. The Friedland bass lines book is a must if you plan to play the bass part in any type of jazz/funk group. The solos are all technically within the reach of any moderately accomplished tuba doubler. The Holmes, Vaughan Williams, and Sowerby solos are lyrical, while the Frackenpohl, Arnold, Lebedev, and Wilder all contain some degree of technical

The Low Brass Player's Guide to Doubling

challenges. The Wilder covers the widest range.

Method Books

Arban, Jean-Baptiste, edited by Dr. Jerry Young and Wesley Jacobs - *Complete Method for Tuba*

Blazhevich, Vladislav - *70 Studies for BB-flat Tuba (two volumes)*

Bordogni, Marco, edited by Wesley Jacobs - *Complete Vocalises for Tuba*

The Complete Boosey and Hawkes Tuba Scale Book

Friedland, Ed - *Building Walking Bass Lines*

Jacobs, Wesley - *Low Register Studies for Tuba*

Kopprasch, C., arranged by Robert King - *60 Selected Studies for BB-flat Tuba*

Parès, Gabriel, revised and edited by Harvey S. Whistler - *Parès Scales for BB-flat Bass*

Snedecor, Phil - *Low Etudes for Tuba*

Tyrell, H.W - *40 Advanced Studies for B-flat Bass*

Solo Repertoire

Arnold, Malcolm - *Fantasy for Tuba*

Frackenpohl, Arthur - *Variations for Tuba and Piano (The Cobbler's Bench)*

Haddad, Don - *Suite for Tuba*

Holmes, Paul – *Lento for Solo Tuba and Piano*

Lebedev, Alexey - *Concerto No. 1 (also known as "Concerto in One Movement")*

Sowerby, Leo - *Chaconne for Tuba and Piano*

Vaughan Williams, Ralph, adapted by Michael Wagner - *Six Studies in English Folksong*

Vaughan, Rodger - *Concertpiece No. 1*

Wilder, Alec - *Suite No. 1 for Tuba and Piano ("Effie Suite")*

Appendix F: Tuba and Cimbasso Resources

Targeted Fundamentals 159

Fingering Charts 171

Overtone Series Charts 179

Chapter 7: Tuba Players Doubling on Euphonium

Alexander Lapins

Why Learn the Euphonium?

Tubists have a variety of reasons to learn to play the euphonium. The euphonium is, after all, a particular type of tenor tuba. Before I learned to play the euphonium, I was called several times each season to cover tenor tuba parts in concerts by orchestras performing works by Holst and Strauss, at which point I had to respectfully explain that tubists do not usually play the tenor tuba. But why not? Why turn down the performance opportunities?

The new trend of more tubists learning the euphonium goes well beyond *The Planets*, however. With the rise of activity in the tuba community over the past fifty years, euphonium players have come along for the ride, even leading to the change in name of our international organization to reflect their significant membership in our community (Tubists Universal Brotherhood Association changed to International Tuba-Euphonium Association). Euphonium players are in no way an auxiliary group to the tuba world; they are equal partners, and the days of people who do not play euphonium but still teach the euphonium might be numbered.

Of course, the primary motivation to learn the euphonium is that it is a magnificent instrument with a magnificent voice and some magnificent repertoire. Learning to play the entire tuba family will also make you a better teacher and a more well-rounded performer.

Treat the Euphonium as Its Own Instrument

The euphonium is a member of the tuba family and shares that basic timbre, but to become truly competent, you must acknowledge that it is its own instrument. Each instrument you play must be mastered on its own terms. This is not to say that when doubling you should not exploit areas where the euphonium and tuba are similar—this is necessary to conserve practice time and avoid duplicative work. Still, it is vital that you also understand how the euphonium and tuba differ from each other so you will make the adjustments needed to achieve maximum success on both instruments. If you choose equipment, repertoire, and sound concept in a way that mimics bass or contrabass tubas too closely, you are missing the unique and beautiful characteristics of the euphonium.

The Low Brass Player's Guide to Doubling

Embouchure Training

The biggest challenge you will likely face in learning the euphonium is the mastery of accuracy, control, and nuance with a more compact embouchure. Even the largest euphonium mouthpieces are significantly smaller than any tuba mouthpiece, and in some ways you have to be willing to go back to basics in the development of embouchure quality, control, and subtle fine-tuning. The most efficient way to do this is through mouthpiece buzzing. Buzzing random pitches or sirens (glissandos between low and high pitches) is an acceptable way to start your practice session, but in the interest of embouchure control, you should buzz specific pitches within specific exercises or melodies as early as possible. Keep a mouthpiece in the car and buzz along with the radio. Buzz along with recorded warm-up routines. The euphonium will seem much less mysterious when you are a master of the euphonium mouthpiece.

Be willing to return to simple, traditional, straightforward brass technical development (see the list of method books at the end of Chapter 5). The Clarke technical studies, Arban interval studies, and Remington flexibility studies are all excellent materials for acclimating yourself to a new brass instrument. Move on to Schlossberg and more modern studies when you are ready, but remember that there are no shortcuts for developing and maintaining excellent playing fundamentals. The Targeted Fundamentals for euphonium in Appendix E provide an excellent and efficient review of euphonium fundamentals, and the solos and method books listed in Chapter 5 provide additional practice material. Practicing scales and arpeggios will further your technical development.

You may at first find it easier to divide your euphonium practice into three shorter sessions each day rather than a single longer session. The smaller mouthpiece and higher tessitura of the euphonium can make practicing taxing at first, even if you are playing in a healthy way.

Developing Proficiency with Fingerings

If your initial playing experience was in an American school band, you almost certainly began your musical life as a tuba player with a BB-flat tuba. Even if you have spent years playing a CC tuba and a bass tuba in F or E-flat, your brain still has memories of thinking in a B-flat fingering pattern, so you only need to remind yourself of and reinforce this ability. While you may have simple exercises from Clarke and Arban memorized on tuba, read them out of the book on euphonium. It is amazing what a few weeks of reading scales can do to establish (or reestablish) reading B-flat fingerings. Sight read many simple melodies daily; explore recent publications of

Concone melodies and other simple bass clef melodies. I am particularly fond of reading jazz tunes out of *The Real Book* and even trying a bit of improvisation daily. The fingering exercises in the aforementioned Targeted Fundamentals provide an additional forum for development and maintenance of euphonium fingering skills.

Holding Position

Most tubists have spent years working toward a playing position that does not strain the body, especially the back, chest, and arms. Devices such as tuba rests are excellent tools for alleviating tension in tuba playing; the ERGObrass for euphonium (discussed in Chapter 5) is an excellent solution for holding a euphonium without tension. It is also possible to use a pillow or to fashion a support out of whatever materials are on hand.

Convention in the euphonium world, however, is to hold up the instrument, cradling it in your left arm, using your right arm only for balance and to manipulate valves. For a tubist who has spent years alleviating muscle involvement in holding up an instrument, it can be an enormous change to hold up an instrument as heavy as a euphonium, especially if you are trying to perform while standing. For this reason, practice seated first to cultivate comfort, balance, breathing, and tone production before moving on to the challenge of playing while standing. The constant use of mirrors to check that your posture is uncompromised while standing to play can help you make this transition in a healthy way. Remember the cardinal rule of brass posture: bring the instrument to you, not the other way around! Once you are able to comfortably make it through your warm-up while standing and holding the instrument, you will likely find that performing literature standing and with the added weight becomes more natural and familiar.

Sound Concept and Manipulation of Wind

The euphonium is its own instrument, with a characteristic sound that is related to that of the tuba but also has unique characteristics. While that has been mentioned before, it is worth considering throughout your exploration of the new instrument. Listen to performances and recordings by the masters of the euphonium as examples and models. A truly world-class euphonium tone has the warmth and roundness of a tuba tone, but with a compact, clarion, crystal-clear aspect, making it an ideal solo instrument. You can only create the tone you can imagine, so model your work after the very best euphonium players. That being said, the claim cannot be made any longer that there is one

The Low Brass Player's Guide to Doubling

"right" tone for euphonium players. Explore the British players, the Japanese, the wide variety of concepts throughout North America, and the rest of the world. Pick what you really like and work toward that goal daily.

Keep an open oral cavity on the euphonium, but experiment with moving from "tOh" to "tAh" to see if you can make the tone more focused and better in tune. I find that I need to keep my oral cavity more or less consistently open moving between tuba and euphonium in order to maintain some consistency in my foundational approach to playing, along with the basic principle of wind as the foundation of brass technique as asserted by Arnold Jacobs. However, this does occasionally cause me to play euphonium with a slightly uninteresting tone and somewhat under pitch. A more compact approach will yield a more in tune result.

You can fine tune your manipulation of wind to each member of the brass family. Moving from tuba to euphonium, keep your wind stream round, warm, and freely flowing, while experimenting with making it more compact. Imagine that the tuba wind stream is akin to moving wind through five straws tied together and on the euphonium it is only three. You still manipulate the airstream with the same basic concepts, only slightly smaller.

Equipment Choices

While the euphonium itself is the largest factor in the equipment area, your transition will be most immediately influenced by the mouthpiece or mouthpieces you select. You will need to find a mouthpiece that best fits both your facial structure and your instrument, prioritizing tone, intonation, and comfort. I suggest you prioritize comfort at first, so you can begin your journey of exploring the new instrument with as much familiarity as possible. Coming from a tuba mouthpiece, this will mean a large euphonium mouthpiece. Using a large bass trombone mouthpiece at first can make for an easier transition, but you might find it difficult to play in tune with the largest mouthpieces. Happily, several manufacturers now make euphonium mouthpieces which are nearly as large as a small bass trombone mouthpiece and yet provide a characteristic tone. These might ultimately prove most comfortable for a tubist doubling on euphonium. With any double, the critical part is getting past the beginning phase. Equipment that makes this early phase easier is certainly a good idea.

There are many factors to consider when purchasing a euphonium. An inexpensive and common instrument such as a Yamaha YEP-321 can be a great choice for your initial efforts, as they are inexpensive, well built, and have decent intonation. However, you may find that a larger euphonium, especially with a large-bore mouthpiece receiver, will make your transition much easier. Furthermore, when considering whether or not to get a compensating euphonium, think about the relative availability of professional-level CC tubas in North America to the availability of professional-level BB-flat tubas. CC tubas are the most common choice of professionals, therefore the great bulk of professional-level contrabass tubas in North America are CC tubas. The same goes for compensating euphoniums: compensating systems are the most common choice of professionals here, so the great majority of available professional euphoniums are compensating. Most tubists are not accustomed to compensating systems, however the fingerings are simpler and it is an easy enough transition to make.

If you prefer to adjust slides as you play tuba to play more easily in tune without compromising your tone with lip-bending, you may find intonation on the euphonium frustrating at first, as manually manipulating slides is difficult or impossible on most models. There is no such thing as a perfectly in tune tuba or euphonium; physics prevents that. However, careful drone work, alternate fingerings (see Chapter 5), and buzzing can get you very close to where you want to be. It is a telling development that over the past dozen years it has become quite common for top-level euphoniums to be fitted with a trigger on the main tuning slide. This primarily is to deal with the sixth partial, but these triggers can make your life much easier throughout the instrument's range, especially when playing in ensembles.

For Further Information

While this chapter should not be approached as a comprehensive guide to the euphonium, I have presented concepts that are most relevant to tubists adding a euphonium double. Again, please refer to Chapter 5 for further information on the subject. While that chapter is directed toward trombonists doubling on euphonium, many of the concepts presented there can be applied equally well by tuba/euphonium doublers, particularly the images, charts, and repertoire listings.

Appendix E: Euphonium and Baritone Horn Resources

Targeted Fundamentals 153

Fingering Chart 156

Overtone Series Chart 158

Chapter 8: Euphonium and Tuba Players Doubling on Trombone

Marc Dickman

Like many euphonium players, I started on trumpet in sixth grade and switched to baritone in seventh grade. Throughout my formative years I stumbled into a doubling career almost by accident, with a series of unexpected opportunities and challenges followed by rapid exploration and practice in order to meet those challenges. This chapter presents a systematic way for euphonium and tuba players to learn how to double on trombone—something from which I would have benefited had it been available to me.

Posture/Holding the Instrument

When playing any trombone, the left hand should support the weight of the instrument, leaving the right hand free to move the slide (see figure 8.1). Avoid supporting the weight of the instrument with the right hand because this will compromise slide technique and cause the slide to become misaligned. The left thumb should wrap around the first bell brace or the F-attachment paddle, the index finger extend across the first slide brace to the mouthpiece receiver, and the remaining three fingers wrap around the lower cork barrel. For bass trombone, the left middle finger will be used in most cases to operate the second valve lever.

Figure 8.1: Left hand holding position

The handslide should be held with the tips of the first and second fingers and thumb of the right hand, with the third and fourth fingers extended, so the entire hand is able to move together without unnecessary tension (see figure 8.2). Strive to use all of the joints of the fingers, hand, wrist, elbow, and shoulder in tandem so that slide motion is quick, efficient, and fluid. A good way to learn this motion is to trace a straight line with the fingers of the right hand.

Figure 8.2: Right hand holding position

Many players touch the bell with the first and second fingers in order to find third position, especially when beginning to play the trombone. This habit should be avoided, as it causes faulty intonation and disrupts otherwise smooth slide movements. One trick to eliminate this habit is to hold a quarter between the fingers and the slide brace. If you try to touch the bell, the coin will fall.

It is very important to hold the handslide using the fingertips rather than closer to the hand (the jointed knuckle area). Holding the handslide correctly makes the smaller joints of the fingers available for fine intonation adjustments, a task for which these joints are far better suited than the elbow or even the wrist. This also promotes a gentle slide action in which gravity and inertia do much of the work, rather than a more muscular approach which is inefficient and can cause both intonation difficulties and slide alignment problems.

While the bass trombone shares the same basic holding position as the tenor, its increased weight can lead to dysfunction and pain, especially since the weight of a double-valve instrument is normally supported by only the fourth and fifth fingers of the left hand. Several solutions to this problem were discussed in Chapter 2; please refer to that discussion if you find yourself having trouble managing the bass trombone.

As with the euphonium and tuba, when playing trombone you must take care to bring the mouthpiece to you, rather than hunching over or otherwise bending or twisting to meet the mouthpiece. Take care not to collapse your arms over your ribs—the arms and elbows should be relaxed and neutral to avoid breathing constriction (see figures 8.3-5).

Figure 8.3: Trombone holding position - standing

Figure 8.4: Trombone holding position - seated

Figure 8.5: Incorrect trombone holding position - hunched over

Choosing an Instrument

The decision to pursue trombone doubling is often an easy one—it is fun to do and can provide a great deal more playing opportunities than playing only euphonium or tuba. However, deciding which trombone to purchase might be difficult, particularly if you intend to perform in multiple genres. If you intend to focus upon the bass trombone, one instrument might be sufficient, but if you choose to play the tenor, you will probably need two instruments to adequately cover every situation. Chapter 3 includes a discussion of the best tenor trombones for different playing situations. To summarize that discussion, a large-bore instrument (.547 inch) is standard equipment for most classical playing, while smaller-bore instruments are usually needed in jazz ensembles. A large-bore instrument can sound nice for jazz soloing in small groups, but it will not be heard over the trumpet and sax sections in a big band. If you want to perform in both classical and jazz idioms as a tenor trombonist, it is advisable to own both large and small-bore instruments.

While modern bass trombones are essentially extra-large-bore tenor trombones, sharing the same slide positions along with the added possibilities provided by the second valve, its larger bore and mouthpiece necessitate that it be treated as a distinct instrument from the tenor. You can choose to

The Low Brass Player's Guide to Doubling

play both, but treat them as separate doubling instruments. If you play both small-bore and large-bore tenor trombones as well as bass trombone, you will essentially be adding three similar yet distinct secondary instruments to your practice and performance responsibilities.

Choosing Mouthpieces

The similar sizes of euphonium and tenor trombone mouthpieces can create a temptation for euphonium players to use the same mouthpiece on both euphonium and tenor trombone. While the two instruments often have the same mouthpiece receivers, a good euphonium mouthpiece usually has a deeper and fuller cup than a good tenor trombone mouthpiece. Your euphonium mouthpiece will probably yield a sound that is too dark and tubby for the trombone. While you will want to use shallower mouthpieces on the tenor trombone than on the euphonium (particularly on the small-bore tenor), look for trombone mouthpieces with a similar diameter to your euphonium mouthpiece in order to minimize embouchure confusion when moving between instruments. You should be able to play euphonium, large-bore tenor, and small-bore tenor on nearly identical rims. That said, you might at least experiment with using a smaller diameter mouthpiece on the small-bore instrument. If you can become accustomed to the change in diameter, you might find that the smaller mouthpiece better facilitates a focused and compact sound.

Bass trombone mouthpieces, on the other hand, will usually be deeper and wider than euphonium mouthpieces. If you use a particularly large euphonium mouthpiece (with a diameter greater than 26.5 mm), you might find that using the same rim for both euphonium and bass trombone works reasonably well, and a few euphonium mouthpieces might be deep enough for the bass trombone if a brighter sound is desired. Normally, though, a deeper cup will be needed to create a full, rich bass trombone sound, and a wider diameter will be necessary to facilitate efficient movement into and out of the pedal register. Using mouthpieces with similar rim contours on both instruments can minimize the discomfort that sometimes accompanies using mouthpieces with different diameters.

Tuba players doubling on bass trombone sometimes try to use a tuba mouthpiece in the bass trombone, and a few manufacturers even make mouthpieces for doublers which combine a tuba rim with a trombone cup. In both cases the result is often unsatisfactory—the sound is uncentered and not characteristic, and intonation difficulties can present themselves. A trombone mouthpiece should be used. The leap from a tuba mouthpiece to a larger bass trombone mouthpiece is not excessively great and is easily managed with practice. Moving from tuba to tenor trombone is a bit more difficult; using a tenor trombone mouthpiece with a larger diameter will ease the transition, as will keeping the same rim when playing both small-bore and large-bore tenor trombones. Tuba players will likely find the excessively small diameters of mouthpieces traditionally associated with small-bore instruments to be uncomfortably restrictive; modular and custom options pairing wider rims with shallow cups can provide a comfortable mouthpiece that yields a characteristic sound.

Mouthpiece choice is always a challenging issue for doublers. The difficulties that attend playing multiple instruments with different mouthpiece requirements can be minimized by using the same rim on different instruments whenever possible, but sometimes using different rims is simply necessary to get the best result. Switching between tuba and trombone almost always includes a change in rim size. You will need to experiment with different setups in order to find the mouthpieces that provide the best sounds and easiest transitions between your different instruments.

Sound Concept

Moving from tuba or euphonium to any of the trombones involves a fairly large shift in sound concept. While the sound of the conical low brasses might be described as dark, warm, and broad, the trombone sound is brighter and more focused. Even the bass trombone's sound will be more compact than that of the tuba. One way to cultivate this sound concept is to think too far in the other direction: when approaching the trombone, think of a trumpet sound. The trombone sound should be in some ways more similar to that of the trumpet than to those of the euphonium or tuba, albeit with a lower pitch and without the same level of brilliance. Listening to the world's greatest trombonists, either live or via recording, will further help you develop your trombone sound concept; many recordings of great players are now available free online, and the regional and international conferences of the International Trombone Association and International Tuba-Euphonium Association provide opportunities to hear and interact with great players on all of your instruments. Taking trombone lessons is recommended, of course, preferably with a teacher who is also a doubler and thus familiar with the switch you are attempting to make. Most of all, playing in ensembles with good trombonists and seeking to emulate their sounds will help you develop and refine your trombone playing. If the section sound is blended and balanced, you are on the right track. Getting a paying gig will be even better—there is no better way to learn and correct your weaknesses on a doubling instrument than in a high-pressure engagement.

The Airstream

All the trombones, including the bass, have smaller bores than any euphonium or tuba. While the large tenor and bass trombones can feel remarkably free-blowing due to the smaller number of bends in the tubing, tuba players in particular will battle a tendency to overblow the trombones, especially the small-bore tenor. The smaller bore sizes and primarily cylindrical tubing of the trombones, combined with the desire for a more focused and direct sound as mentioned above, requires tuba and euphonium players to reduce the airflow and focus on using a smaller and more compact airstream. If you feel the instrument backing up, simply reduce the airflow. This will probably feel a bit strange at first, but remember to prize sound concept over feel. As the saying goes, "if it sounds good, it is good." The unfamiliar feeling will diminish over time.

Slide Positions

Euphonium and BB-flat tuba players will find moving to tenor or bass trombone relatively simple because there is a correlation between fingerings and slide positions as illustrated on the following chart. There is, of course, an octave displacement involved when moving between tuba and trombone, and CC, E-flat, and F tuba players will have to introduce an extra step when thinking of trombone positions in this way. The slide positions with no letters preceding them are those with no valves engaged, those preceded by an F are with the F-attachment engaged, and likewise for the G-flat and D (combined valves) attachments.

Euphonium and BB-flat Tuba Fingerings (Non-Compensating)	Euphonium and BB-flat Tuba Fingerings (Compensating)	Tenor Trombone with F Attachment Slide Positions	Bass Trombone (F/G-flat/D) Slide Positions
Open	Open	1	1
2	2	2	2
1	1	3	3
1-2, or 3	1-2, or 3	4	4
2-3	2-3	5	5, or G♭1
4, or 1-3	4, or 1-3	6, or F1	6, F1, or G♭2
2-4, or 1-2-3	2-4, or 1-2-3	7, or F2	7, F2, or G♭3
1-4, or 1-2-4	1-4	F3	F3, or G♭4
2-3-4	1-2-4	F4	F4, G♭5, or D1
1-3-4	2-3-4	F5	F5, G♭6, or D2
1-2-3-4	1-3-4	F6	F6, or D3
1-2-3-4-5	1-2-3-4	Not Present	D4

The function of the F-attachment is roughly analogous to that of the fourth valve on euphonium and tuba, while the added valve on most bass trombones gives the instrument a fully chromatic low register and introduces a plethora of additional fingering possibilities.

While this chart can provide a basic comprehension of slide positions relative to the fingerings on your primary instrument, learning the overtone charts for your trombones (provided in Appendix C and D) will further your understanding and skill.

It is important to understand that trombone slide positions are not equidistant (see figure 8.6). The farther out you go, the farther away the next slide position is.

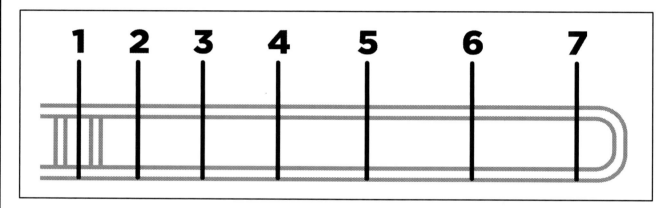

Figure 8.6: Trombone slide positions

This phenomenon continues as you add tubing by engaging valves. For example, with the F attachment valve engaged, there are only six slide positions because each position must be proportionally farther out than the last (see figure 8.7)

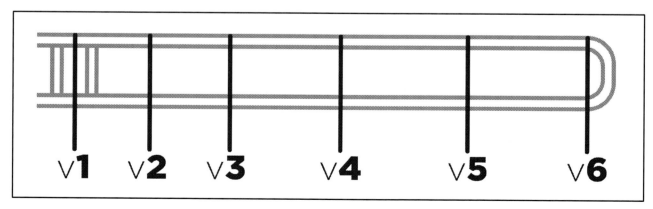

Figure 8.7: Trombone slide positions with F attachment

When using both valves together, there are only five slide positions (see figure 8.8).

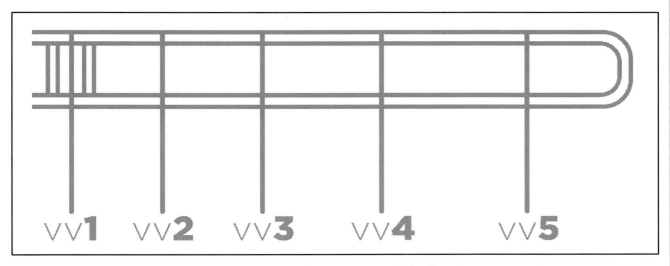

Figure 8.8: Trombone slide positions with both valves engaged

These tendencies must be accounted for when playing. Third position with the F attachment engaged is farther out than normal third position, for example. Generally speaking, as you add valves, also add length to the slide position. Figure 8.9 gives a composite accounting of these differences.

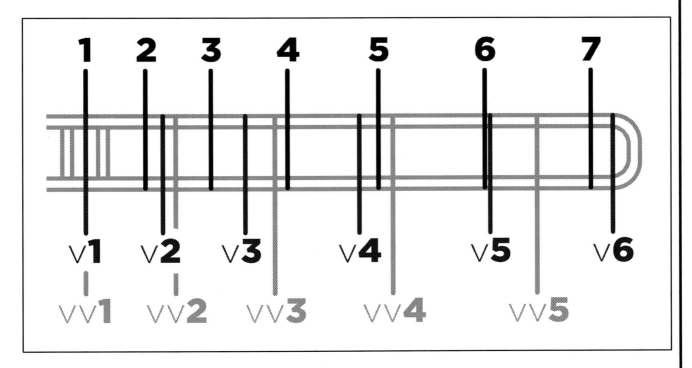

Figure 8.9: Relationships of trombone slide positions

The Low Brass Player's Guide to Doubling

Using the Handslide and Valve(s)

Trombone slide technique is simple enough in concept, though mastering it can be tricky. Make sure you are using a proper right hand position as noted above, and that the shoulder, elbow, wrist, and fingers work together in moving the slide. Rely more on the wrist and fingers for smaller movements, especially when making fine intonation adjustments. The elbow and shoulder are needed for larger motions, but are poorly suited for smaller ones. Use the body in the most efficient way possible. A good way to cultivate efficiency is to trace a straight line with the fingers of your right hand all the way out to seventh position and back. When moving the slide in this way, you should see a minimal amount of bell movement, with a correspondingly small amount of disruption to the embouchure as the result of the mouthpiece moving on the face.

While the slide is held between the thumb and first two fingers of the right hand, the grip should not be overly tight but rather have a certain amount of play between the thumb and fingers. This enables you to guide the slide along its track and allow you to make quick motions without jerking the instrument or bending the slide tubes. The slide must be kept clean, well-lubricated, and in good repair for this to work. The most fragile part of the trombone is also the most exposed—take care to protect the slide.

Operating the valves on instruments so equipped is relatively straightforward. The first valve is almost always operated with the left thumb using a very simple action. The second valve on modern double-valve bass trombones is operated with the left middle finger, though on some older instruments it might also be operated with the thumb. In both cases, the valve operation itself is simple, though managing the second valve can be a challenge. With a thumb valve, the difficulty is in operating two levers with only one thumb. Valves operated with the middle finger can lead to difficulties with balance and weight management. Refer to Chapter 2 for suggested solutions to these difficulties.

Once you are holding and operating the instrument correctly, daily practice of scales, arpeggios, and technical exercises from method books by Clarke, Arban, and others will help solidify slide and valve technique. Use a metronome, start slowly, and strive to play accurately, increasing speed only when you can accurately execute the passages. Joining an ensemble on your new instrument will not only promote tone quality but will spur improvements in technical skill as well.

The use of alternate positions is an important part of developing fine trombone slide technique. These positions are more frequently necessary and useful on the trombone than alternate fingerings

81

on the euphonium or tuba. You might choose to use alternate positions to make slide movements more fluid (i.e. changing direction less frequently), to facilitate lip slurring across partials, or even to achieve a particular timbre or tuning effect such as keeping two notes in a leading tone-tonic relationship in a single partial in order to maintain a consistent tone quality. In many cases the use of one or more alternate positions will not only be possible but necessary for the correct and efficient execution of a passage. For this reason, I have taken to referring to these not as alternate positions but as "better" positions.

The importance of these better positions is an additional reason to develop a thorough familiarity with the overtone series chart for the instrument you are playing. The better you know the overtone series for each position, the more fingering possibilities will be available to you. If you have also memorized the tuning tendencies of each partial, you will be able to employ myriad possible slide positions with little or no detrimental effect on tone quality or pitch. For example, if you are playing a passage consisting largely of lower-register notes in outer slide positions

Figure 8.10: Using "F" in sixth position instead of first position to improve slide technique

you might elect to play the entire passage in outer positions. Playing F in sixth position is common in such situations (see figure 8.10) and is often the first alternate position learned by young trombonists. If you have an F-attachment you might choose to play B-flat in F3 and (less commonly) A in F4, for similar reasons (see figure 8.11). Playing middle and even upper-register notes in outer positions also becomes necessary when executing some glissandi.

Figure 8.11: Using the F attachment to improve slide technique

Sometimes trombonists will also use alternate positions to keep the slide moving in the same direction through most or all of a phrase. One often finds that eliminating back-and-forth motions of the slide leads to a smoother legato, even if this means using a legato tongue where a lip slur could otherwise be used (see figure 8.12).

As mentioned previously, keeping leading tone-tonic relationships within the same partial leads to better tuning and timbral consistency, even when alternate positions are used. In the key of B major, for example, playing A-sharp 3 in fifth position rather than first can improve that pitch's "leading" to the B in fourth.

Figure 8.12: Using D in flat four instead of first to improve slide technique

Intonation

Every brass instrument operates according to the principles of the overtone series, and the various partials have the same tuning tendencies. Likewise, the tendencies of different chord tones are the same regardless of the instrument being played. If you know the partial of a note in a given position and its place in the chord sounding at a given moment, you will know the tuning adjustment that is most likely needed.

The difference between tuning on the euphonium or tuba and tuning on the trombone lies not in which adjustments are needed, but in how those adjustments are made. Valve instrument players are most accustomed to correcting intonation by bending or lipping pitches with the embouchure, with alternate fingerings and tuning slide adjustments used secondarily. The trombone, though, is a giant tuning slide, and practically all tuning adjustments should be made using fine movements of the handslide. With practice, along with careful use of a tuner, you will find that practically every note has its own unique slide position, which is itself further adjusted depending upon the needs of a particular piece or ensemble. Playing simple songs by ear in all keys will further improve intonation by enhancing the connection between hand and ear.

Adjusting pitch using the embouchure is not recommended on the trombone. The instrument does not respond as well as the euphonium or tuba to being played outside of the center of a given partial, and such adjustments are unnecessary due to the adjustments made possible by the handslide.

Articulation

The trombone, euphonium, and tuba share the same basic articulation technique, though there are slight differences which must be understood and mastered. The single biggest difference is that true

The Low Brass Player's Guide to Doubling

slurring is impossible on the trombone, except when crossing partials. This makes the development of a refined legato tonguing technique vitally important if you are to be successful as a trombone doubler.

While many method books teach legato tonguing solely by prescribing a softer tonguing technique (i.e. "dah" instead of "tah"), the maintenance of a constant airstream is even more important for producing a good legato (and for good slurring on the euphonium or tuba). To play legato on the trombone, blow a steady stream of air and use quick tongue strikes at the beginnings of notes to avoid unwanted glissandi. Where natural slurs are possible, the tongue is not needed, though you might choose to use the legato tongue even when it is not absolutely necessary if this yields a better result in a given situation.

A good legato requires that the slide action be both quick and smooth. Think of it this way: the legato tongue is used in order to avoid unwanted glissandi. If this is to be successful, you will need to move the slide from one position to the other during the split-second during which the air/buzz is disrupted by the tongue (or, with natural slurs, by the partial break). Take care not to jerk the handslide, though, as this will create an unwanted articulation of its own. Remember to hold the slide gently and to guide it along its track, using gravity and inertia to do some of the work rather than brute force.

For other articulations, euphonium players will likely find that the tongue strike for a given pitch and articulation will need to be somewhat softer on the trombone than on the euphonium. The transition between tuba and trombone will be less pronounced. In every case, use your ears—again, "if it sounds good, it is good."

Clefs

Bass trombone music is almost always written in concert pitch and in bass clef. If you plan to limit your trombone doubling to the bass trombone, learning a new clef will probably not be necessary. Tenor trombone music, however, is frequently written in tenor clef and occasionally in alto clef. Those doubling on tenor trombone will need to become very proficient reading tenor clef, and moderately so with alto clef. The method book by Brad Edwards listed below will help you develop reading skills in both clefs, developing proficiency and ear training by finding unknown notes via their intervallic relationships with more familiar ones. Playing in ensembles with tenor or alto clef parts, particularly trombone ensembles which frequently use those clefs in multiple parts,

The Low Brass Player's Guide to Doubling

will provide even more help. Euphonium players familiar with treble clef parts will find the transition to tenor clef to be relatively easy—the music looks the same, and if desired can be read as if it were in B-flat treble clef by adding two sharps to or subtracting two flats from the key signature, along with related adjustments to accidentals on written B's and E's.

While gaining thorough mastery of tenor and alto clefs is desirable, writing at least a few note names and fingerings in the part is sometimes necessary when learning a new clef or instrument. This should become less frequent as your proficiency increases.

Mutes

Euphonium and tuba players doubling on trombone will discover that trombone parts demand mutes much more frequently than do parts for their primary instruments. Straight and cup mutes might suffice for those playing primarily in classical idioms, but any playing in jazz, musical theater, or other popular idioms will probably require Harmon, plunger, and bucket mutes, and perhaps even pixie, solotone, or other types of mutes. The relationship between mute and instrument is usually less particular with the trombones than with the euphonium or tuba, but those playing both tenor and bass trombones will need separate sets of mutes for each. In some cases small-bore and large-bore tenor trombones will require different mutes, particularly with cup and bucket mutes.

Suggested Practice and Performance Literature

The Arban and Clarke books are great for developing technique and internalizing regular patterns. The newer edition of the Arban is particularly good, as it lays flat on your music stand and has fewer mistakes and omissions than earlier editions. The Bordogni book is an effective way of developing both phrasing and legato playing, which is not as carefree on the trombone as on the euphonium. Mastering the legato tongue is a high priority! The Edwards book is a great tool for learning clefs and for teaching your brain to "change gears" between them. The bass trombone methods by Paul Faulise and Alan Raph are effective introductions to the double-valve bass trombone. The volumes by McChesney, Waits, and Raph and Steinmeyer introduce styles and techniques for jazz and commercial music—genres which are sometimes unfamiliar to euphonium and tuba players. The doodle tonguing technique explored by McChesney is occasionally useful in classical genres, as well. The solos listed here are great for those new to the trombones; additional solo works are listed in Chapters 2 and 3.

Method Books

Arban, Jean-Baptiste, edited by Joseph Alessi and Dr. Brian Bowman - *Complete Method for Trombone and Euphonium*

Bordogni, Giulio Marco, annotated and edited by Michael Mulcahy - *Complete Vocalises for Trombone*

Bordogni, Giulio Marco, arranged and edited by Allen Ostrander - *Melodious Etudes for Bass Trombone*

Clarke, Herbert L., edited by Claude Gordon - *Technical Studies for Bass Clef Instruments*

Edwards, Brad - *Introductory Studies in Tenor and Alto Clef for Trombone "Before Blazhevich"*

Faulise, Paul - *The F&D Double-Valve Bass Trombone*

Kopprasch, Georg, edited by Keith Brown - *60 Studies for Trombone* (2 vols.)

McChesney, Bob - *Doodle Studies and Etudes*

Raph, Alan and Dave Steinmeyer - *Beyond Boundaries*

Raph, Alan - *The Double-Valve Bass Trombone*

Remington, Emory, prepared and edited by Donald Hunsberger - *The Remington Warm-Up Studies*

Schlossberg, Max, edited by C.K. Schlossberg - *Daily Drills and Technical Studies for Trombone*

Waits, Greg - *Advanced Flexibility Studies for the Jazz Trombonist*

Solo Repertoire

Tenor Trombone

Barat, J. Ed. - *Andante et Allegro for Trombone and Piano*

Guilmant, Alexandre, arranged by E. Falaguerra - *Morceau Symphonique*

Hasse, Johann Adolph, compiled and edited by Wm. Gower - *Hasse Suite*

Rimsky-Korsakov, Nicolai - *Trombone Concerto*

Telemann, Georg Philipp, edited by Allen Ostrander and Robert Veyron-Lecroix - *Sonata in F Minor*

Bass Trombone

Hoffman, Earl - *Trigger Treat*

Lieb, Richard - *Concertino Basso*

McCarty, Patrick - *Sonata for Bass Trombone*

Raph, Alan - *Rock*

Semler-Collery, Jules - *Barcarolle et Chanson Bachique*

Appendix C: Bass Trombone Resources

Targeted Fundamentals 135

Fingering Charts 141

Overtone Series Charts 145

Appendix D: Tenor Trombone Resources

Targeted Fundamentals 147

Fingering Chart 150

Overtone Series Chart 152

Chapter 9: Alto Trombone

Prior to a renaissance beginning in the 1970s, the alto trombone had been regarded as little more than a historical curiosity. Trombonists knew it existed, but few were inclined to play it and instruments were not readily available. An increased interest in historical accuracy, combined with a renewed appreciation of the alto trombone's timbre in certain contexts, has led to the alto trombone becoming a necessary double for those occupying principal chairs in symphony orchestras. Alto trombones have been manufactured in the keys of E-flat, F, and perhaps others, but the E-flat instrument is most common and will be discussed in this chapter.

The reintroduction of the alto trombone has added a helpful color to the orchestral palette, particularly for Classical and early Romantic works. The high tessitura of the first trombone parts in works by Haydn, Mozart, Beethoven, and their contemporaries is much easier to negotiate on the alto trombone than on the tenor, due to the instrument's ready high register response and to the notes occupying a lower position in the overtone series on the alto than on the tenor. The skilled player is less likely to mistakenly find an adjacent partial when playing in this range on the alto trombone, and the more compact sound of the alto is particularly effective in the smaller orchestras often employed when performing this repertoire. An entire section of smaller instruments, using an alto trombone on the first part, a small-bore tenor trombone on the second part, and a large-bore tenor trombone on the bass part, is much more appropriate for such works than the larger instruments used for later works requiring greater orchestral forces. This is most evident in works such as the *Great C Major Symphony* by Franz Schubert, in which the trombones often provide supporting chordal material at soft volumes.

Determining whether or not to use the alto trombone in the orchestra becomes more difficult with certain Romantic-period works. First trombone parts are often labeled as alto trombone and printed in alto clef regardless of the instrument intended, so labeling is a poor guide to instrumentation. Many players will choose to use alto trombone for works by Felix Mendelssohn-Bartholdy but not those by Hector Berlioz. The volume levels required for modern performances of the latter composer's works make using the alto trombone inadvisable even for parts that appear to have been written with the smaller instrument in mind. Questionable cases are best left to the discretion of the conductor. For example, some conductors prefer the alto trombone for the first parts in symphonies by Johannes Brahms, while others will insist upon the tenor.

The eighteenth century was a fertile period for the alto trombone in solo and chamber works, as well. Trombonists and musicologists have unearthed a number of period works calling for skilled soloistic playing on the alto trombone, including concerti by Johann Georg Albrechtsberger and Georg Christoph Wagenseil, divertimenti by Leopold Mozart and Johann Michael Haydn, and even an obbligato alto trombone part in an early work by Wolfgang Amadeus Mozart. Surviving works by less prominent composers calling for the alto trombone in chamber contexts are relatively abundant, particularly from Vienna and its immediate vicinity. While much of this music can be played on the tenor trombone, the sound is often inappropriately big. Mastering the alto trombone brings this interesting music into the player's repertoire, providing audiences at low brass recitals with a needed break in programs otherwise populated entirely with more recent works. Since these early pieces were originally written for trombone, they make an attractive alternative to playing arrangements of pieces originally for cello, bassoon, or other instruments.

Perhaps the most important reason to double on alto trombone is simply that it sounds good. Whether the original orchestration for Mozart's *Requiem* included an E-flat alto trombone or B-flat tenor trombone on first trombone, I use the E-flat instrument because it provides the sound and response I want for that piece. Likewise with the Albrechtsberger *Concerto*—the easier ornamentation on the B-flat instrument notwithstanding, I prefer the sound of the E-flat instrument, so that is what I use. While concern for historical accuracy might have been partially responsible for the resurgence of the E-flat alto trombone in recent decades, players continue to use it because it yields the desired sound on these works, and conductors have begun to call for it for the same reason. For early solo, chamber, and orchestral works—as well as for an increasing number of works by more recent composers—the alto trombone is a useful and often necessary double.

Sound Concept

Because nearly every player doubling on alto trombone primarily plays a larger instrument with a bigger sound and greater air requirements—usually but not always the tenor trombone—those new to the alto trombone have a tendency to overblow the instrument. Even more experienced doublers often battle this tendency. Blowing more air than the instrument can accommodate causes the air to back up and the player's aperture to become too large. The resulting sound is diffuse and uncentered, and the excessive separation between the lips leads to response problems. Developing a proper sound concept is a vital part of eliminating these difficulties.

The Low Brass Player's Guide to Doubling

The simplest and most effective way of conceiving a characteristic alto trombone sound is to think of it as a big trumpet sound (after all, the word "trombone" comes to us from the Italian term meaning "big trumpet"). Trombones and trumpets both have primarily cylindrical tubing and share similar characteristic sounds, and the alto trombone is pitched almost exactly halfway between the B-flat trumpet and the tenor trombone, so it makes sense that the timbre of the alto trombone also would occupy a place between those of the trumpet and tenor trombone.

The player who adopts this trumpet-like sound concept will use somewhat less air and a more compact and focused airstream, almost without thinking. The aforementioned overblowing problem is thus solved and the resulting sound is both pleasing and characteristic to the instrument. Consulting recordings of skilled alto trombone players is advisable to further cultivate your tone. The goal is to make it difficult for the uninformed listener to tell whether the instrument being played is a dark trumpet or a light trombone.

Mastering New Slide Positions

As is the case with the other trombones, the alto trombone has seven positions (with an additional six for instruments with a B-flat attachment), with the distance between positions getting progressively longer as one moves farther down the slide. Initially, finding these positions can be more difficult on the alto trombone than on the tenor, as the various visual and tactile clues used to help beginning students find positions on the tenor trombone do not always apply on the alto. Some alto trombones are constructed in such a way that the relative locations of the bell and slide are similar to those on the tenor trombone, which can help in locating third and fourth positions. Other instruments are not constructed in this way, and on no alto trombone is seventh position as far as you can reach—most players have the frightening experience of going off the end of the slide several times before becoming fully aware of the correct location of seventh position on the alto trombone. Of course, your ears are the best tools for finding the correct location of any position and any adjustments needed in a particular circumstance.

Finding positions is one challenge; learning which notes are played in those positions is another. The player who understands the overtone series and its application to all brass instruments has a great advantage in learning this skill. The series of notes available in each position on the alto trombone is a perfect fourth higher than those on the tenor trombone. Not only do the intervallic relationships between partials remain constant from one instrument to the next, but the tuning

90

The Low Brass Player's Guide to Doubling

tendencies of each partial remain so, as well. Based on this understanding alone, a skilled player can devise fundamental exercises and scale studies which will aid in finding the positions more directly, and not simply by comparison to the tenor trombone.

At this point the player faces a decision: should you approach the alto trombone as a transposing instrument, using methods and exercises with the sounding pitch a perfect fourth higher than the written pitch, or should you strive from the beginning to read and execute music written in concert pitch? While there are certain method books and even a few editions of solo works which take the former approach, I recommend only the latter. Music for alto trombone is practically always written in concert pitch using alto clef. Using the crutch of reading transposed music prepares you to read a type of written music that does not exist in the real world. This will unnecessarily delay your development of the ability to read—and especially sight-read—the parts you will be called upon to play on the alto trombone. It is better to face the difficulty of reading in concert pitch from the very beginning. The learning curve may be a bit steeper, but you will more quickly become a competent working alto trombonist this way.

In addition to performing scale studies and Targeted Fundamentals on the alto trombone, I recommend using the *Method for Alto Trombone* by Branimir Slokar. This method presents a two-week program of exercises that, if followed as prescribed, will provide a functional ability to read and execute written music on the alto trombone.

Playing duets is a good way to refine your tuning on the new instrument. Playing along with a friend who has a good sense of pitch is best, though a workable alternative is to play duets alone by recording one part and playing the other part along with the recording. The use of recorded drones is similarly helpful.

Choosing an Instrument

Manufacturers often take one of two approaches when designing and marketing alto trombones: build a quality alto trombone for its own sake, usually with a fairly small bore and bell and with relative locations of bell and slide that might or might not be similar to that on the tenor trombone; or design an alto trombone that is as similar as possible to the tenor trombone and explicitly market it as such. The second type of instrument will usually have a larger bore and bell than the first type, and the bell flare is purposefully placed so the locations of third and fourth positions relative to the bell are the same as on the tenor trombone. The first type of instrument will most readily yield a characteristic alto trombone sound in the hands of a player with a good sound concept and approach to blowing, though the initial learning curve might be steeper because it is not as similar to a tenor trombone. The second type of instrument is less subject to being overblown by the inexperienced player and its slide positions are easier to find, but producing a characteristically compact alto trombone timbre can be more difficult. This description of two types of alto trombone provides a helpful paradigm for evaluating instruments.

The reintroduction of tuning in the slide mechanisms by some high-end makers (see figure 9.1) has facilitated the creation of small-bore instruments with a characteristically light sound that are remarkably free-blowing due to their conical bell sections. If you have a large budget for purchasing an alto trombone, this

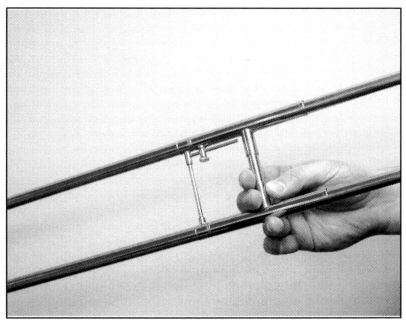

Figure 9.1: Alto trombone with tuning in the slide mechanism

type of instrument might be the best choice. Those looking for a more affordable entry-level model will likely find instruments that tend toward one of the two extremes just described.

Other equipment options include a B-flat attachment and a half-step trill valve. The B-flat attachment extends the lower register of the instrument a perfect fourth in the same way the F-attachment does on tenor and bass trombones, allowing the player to avoid using sixth and seventh positions. This can be helpful in facilitating technique and avoiding the danger of dropping the outer slide. The B-flat attachment also facilitates playing whole-step lip trills in the lower part of the range without moving the slide—an important consideration given the highly ornamented nature of the eighteenth-century literature. The half-step trill valve enables the execution of half-step trills, practically all of which are impossible on a straight alto trombone (one without a valve) without moving the slide, and only a few of which are available on an instrument with a B-flat attachment.

Alto trombone valves are sometimes placed so they press into players' necks or jaws, causing

The Low Brass Player's Guide to Doubling

discomfort and possible disruption in the operation of the valve. Those considering purchasing an alto trombone with either type of valve should consider this issue carefully; both types of valves provide certain advantages but neither is absolutely necessary.

Choosing a Mouthpiece

The mouthpiece used with the alto trombone should be smaller than that used with all but the smallest tenor trombones, given the alto's characteristically brighter and more compact sound. The question is whether to use an alto trombone mouthpiece with the same rim as your primary instrument mouthpiece—with a shallow cup and a backbore more suitable for the alto—or one which is smaller in all of its dimensions. Using the same rim on multiple instruments lessens the sometimes unpleasant sensation of changing embouchures when moving from one instrument to another, and has the advantage of allowing you to use your embouchure muscles in a similar way on each instrument. The mouthpieces traditionally used for playing alto trombone have a diameter of less than one inch—a small size which players with fleshier lips might find unmanageable. However, using a mouthpiece with a wider rim will increase the likelihood of overblowing the instrument; a mouthpiece with a smaller diameter helps to promote the more compact approach required by the alto.

Pitfalls to Avoid

Here are five potential pitfalls alto trombone doublers need to avoid:

1. Overblowing the instrument. Players tend to use too much air when doubling on alto, a problem which often persists throughout one's career. Writing reminders to blow correctly on your alto trombone sheet music or elsewhere in the practice space is an effective way to ensure that correct blowing technique, once mastered, is actively maintained.

2. Thinking "in B-flat." Most alto trombone doublers are primarily tenor trombonists, so those players tend to learn the new alto trombone slide positions by relating them to the tenor trombone slide positions. For example, to find the position for D4 on the alto trombone, the player would think of the note that is a perfect fourth lower (A3) and the slide position for that note on the tenor trombone (second position). Because the slide positions of the alto trombone are the same as those of the tenor transposed up a perfect fourth, the slide position for A3 on the tenor trombone will be the position for D4 on the alto. While thinking in this way is expected and even helpful when first beginning alto trombone study, continuing to rely on this crutch will hinder the development of your playing and particularly your sight reading on the alto trombone. Additionally, maintaining this constant transposition process will keep you from being fully aware of what note you are playing, its tuning tendency within the overtone series, and its melodic and harmonic place within the ensemble. This pitfall is essentially a failure to genuinely learn the alto trombone's slide positions.

3. *Poor intonation.* Next to overblowing, poor intonation is probably the most common pitfall. While the transposition issue mentioned above is a potential cause of this, the culprit is more often a failure to accurately locate the slide positions on the alto trombone. While the distances between positions on the alto trombone are proportionally similar to those on the tenor, the alto's shorter slide means that those distances are all shorter. Mastering the shorter slide will require you to trust your ear at first and develop over time an unconscious tactile sense of each position's location, just as on the other trombones.

4. *Expecting high register miracles.* Players adding a smaller and higher pitched doubling instrument sometimes assume the new instrument will yield vast improvements in the high range. This expectation will likely be unfulfilled; the *player* produces the buzz, not the instrument, and if you cannot buzz a high note on one instrument, that ability is unlikely to manifest itself on another. A skilled player will indeed be able to produce the high notes already available on a larger instrument with greater ease on the alto trombone, and with a better sound. This benefit is not automatic, though, and players who have not yet mastered the correct usage of the airstream on the alto trombone will sometimes find their upper register response is actually poorer on the alto. The alto trombone brings with it the *potential* for great upper register playing, but diligent work is still needed for this potential to be realized.

5. *Failure to actively maintain alto playing ability.* Despite its pleasing sound and undeniable utility in certain situations, the alto trombone is one of the more infrequently requested low brass instruments. Principal players in symphony orchestras with full seasons might be called upon to play alto a few times a year; once a year or even twice every three years are more common scenarios for

The Low Brass Player's Guide to Doubling

those in regional orchestras giving fewer concerts. The alto trombone will not be needed very much unless you create opportunities to play it by organizing solo recitals, chamber music concerts, etc. This rarity of usage brings with it the temptation to neglect alto trombone practice during the down times. While most players should be able to reduce regular alto trombone practice to a minimal amount of maintenance work (Targeted Fundamentals) during such periods, putting the instrument away entirely until shortly before it is needed is inadvisable. The redevelopment of alto trombone skills after a period of neglect requires longer and more frustrating practice sessions than are needed to merely move the instrument from the back burner to a place of more active use. Besides, if the phone rings with a last minute alto trombone gig, you want to be able to take the job and play well.

Suggested Practice and Performance Literature

The following listing is not comprehensive, but should provide a good start for your alto trombone studies, provided that the suggested Targeted Fundamentals and scale and arpeggio studies are practiced regularly. The particular value of the Slokar volume and of practicing duets (such as the simple ones found in the Arban book) has already been mentioned. While the solo repertoire listed consists entirely of works intended for the alto trombone, as does the Shifrin and Longstaff excerpt book, most of the method books listed here were not originally written for the alto trombone. Nevertheless, the Fink book can provide some helpful work on notes and positions after completion of the Slokar volume, while the more challenging Maxted book is primarily in alto clef and provides a fine workout for the alto trombonist. Players without B-flat attachments will need to make certain adjustments in tonal range. The Arban and Bordogni books always provide helpful technical and lyrical studies though range adjustments will sometimes be necessary when using these with the alto trombone. Practicing materials not in alto clef on the alto trombone will help to further solidify your grasp of the instrument.

Method Books

Arban, Jean-Baptiste, edited by Joseph Alessi and Dr. Brian Bowman - *Complete Method for Trombone and Euphonium*

Bordogni, Giulio Marco, annotated and edited by Michael Mulcahy - *Complete Vocalises for Trombone*

Fink, Reginald H. - *Introducing the Alto Clef for Trombone*

Maxted, George - *Twenty Studies for Tenor Trombone*

Shifrin, Ken and Danny Longstaff - *The Professional's Handbook of Orchestral Excerpts: Alto Trombone*

Slokar, Branimir - *Method for Alto Trombone*

Solo Repertoire

Albrechtsberger, Johann Georg, edited by Gábor Darvas and Jenő Vécsey - *Concerto for Alto Trombone and Orchestra*

Anonymous, edited by Christian Lindberg - *Three Medieval Dances*

Finger, Gottfried, edited by Miloslav Hejda and Jaroslav Mašталir - *Sonata in E-flat*

Haydn, Johann Michael, edited by Randy Kohlenberg - *Concerto for Alto Trombone—Extracted from Divertimento in D (1764)*

Mozart, Leopold, edited by Alexander Weinmann - *Concerto for Alto Trombone or Viola and Orchestra*

Wagenseil, Georg Christoph, edited by Paul Bryan - *Concerto for Trombone*

Appendix G: Alto Trombone Resources

Targeted Fundamentals 183

Fingering Chart 186

Overtone Series Chart 188

Chapter 10: Contrabass Trombone

Jeffrey Cortazzo

Why Play the Contrabass Trombone?

This is a great question, especially given the limited opportunities for using the instrument in a situation where one would actually be compensated. Still, with the proliferation of trombone choirs and the relative availability of high quality instruments, the question really becomes, "Why not play the contrabass trombone?"

As musicians, we should continually seek to improve ourselves. Taking on a new challenge is not a foreign concept to those in the music business. Indeed, we are almost obligated by our philosophies to seek out new modes of expression. Learning and playing contrabass trombone fits this concept nicely. The contra can add an unmatched depth to any ensemble and, when played well, gives the player a unique skillset that few others possess. As an added bonus, playing the contrabass trombone can improve your skill on your primary instrument.

Initial Approach

When comparing the tenor and alto trombones, the differences between the sounds of the two instruments are generally known to trombonists, given the interval of a perfect fourth between the

Figure 10.1: F/D/BB-flat/AA-flat contrabass trombone

The Low Brass Player's Guide to Doubling

fundamental pitches of the two instruments. Their respective timbres, slide techniques, articulation techniques, etc. are fundamentally related, yet distinctive. The contrabass trombone (in F) is pitched a perfect fourth lower than the bass trombone. The basis of comparison is thus the same as that between the tenor and alto, but in the opposite direction. Thus the challenge for a bass trombonist learning the contrabass is nearly the same as that of a tenor trombonist learning the alto trombone for the first time. Those taking up a contra double should understand that it will take significant effort for it to feel somewhat natural, but also that the rewards of the timbre and sonic presence this instrument affords are well worth the effort.

I received my contrabass trombone during the early summer, a time of year when my performing schedule is rather intense and my individual practice time severely limited. I therefore devoted practically all my individual practice time for the entire summer to learning the contra. This "full immersion" approach really helped me to begin thinking in F, and to play the contrabass trombone as its own instrument rather than merely a departure from the bass trombone. I therefore recommend that when taking up the contra you devote a significant portion of your practice time to the effort. Do not worry—you will not forget the bass or tenor trombones when learning the contra. On the contrary, your skills on those instruments might very well improve. At least that was my experience —ever since taking up the contra my double-pedal D-flat, C, B, and B-flat practically fall out of the horn, even on the bass trombone. Evidently, the contra showed me where these notes are on my face!

Sound Concept

While the timbre of the contrabass trombone is unique, it should still sound like a trombone—the lowest, most glorious trombone in existence! Happily, the long cylindrical spans and carefully controlled tapers largely prevent the production of a sound that is excessively tuba-like. Remember that the contrabass trombone in F is really just a bass trombone—some would say the "true" bass trombone, compared to the modern bass trombone which is essentially an extra-large-bore tenor trombone—so in every respect, the contra is *played* like a trombone and should therefore *sound* like one.

Choosing an Instrument

There are many brands of contrabass trombone from which to choose, each offering unique materials, valve configurations, and tonal characteristics. Given the usual necessity of special-ordering a contrabass trombone directly from the factory, your best bet for trying different makes, models, and options is to visit one of the many trombone festivals held throughout the world and try instruments in the exhibit hall. Contact the manufacturers in advance to make sure they plan to bring their contrabass trombones to the event. You might also try to find someone who owns a contra and ask to borrow or rent it for a few weeks. These steps will help you to become more familiar with the instrument and to make an informed determination of the configuration which will best suit your needs.

Of course, economic realities might do much to determine your choice. At the time of writing, only one American manufacturer, Kanstul, makes a contrabass trombone, while a number of European manufacturers do so. International exchange rates often render the better European instruments too costly for American players. The Kanstul contrabass trombone is an F/C/D-flat/AA instrument, so the open horn and the valves are all a perfect fourth below the usual B-flat/F/G-flat/D bass trombone. Many players find this exact mirroring of the bass trombone a perfect fourth lower eases the transition between the two instruments. Another common configuration, found on instruments by Thein and others, is intended to yield an easy transition in a different way. By building their instruments in F/D/BB-flat/AA-flat, these manufacturers have made an instrument in which the open horn and the two valves independently have slide positions that are very similar to those on the bass trombone, while the valves combined add a few additional low-register fingerings.

While these two configurations are common (and are the ones for which we have provided exercises and charts in Appendix H), a number of others are available. Indeed, since the contrabass trombone is usually a special-order item, practically any valve configuration desired by the player can be obtained. As you consider contrabass trombones for purchase, try as many instruments as possible and seek to identify the characteristics and valve configuration which best suits your playing.

Before leaving this discussion of instrument selection, the BB-flat contrabass trombone, which is pitched one octave below the bass trombone, is worth mentioning. This instrument has a double-wrapped slide (four pairs of tubes instead of two) and a valve/bell section which is also double-wrapped, giving it roughly the same visual profile as a standard bass trombone. Ironically, this instrument feels less "like a trombone" than the F contra, due in part to the fundamental being so low. There is also a great deal of resistance due to the mostly cylindrical bore. With the right mouthpiece, this instrument performs well and is capable of making the lowest notes of the piano

The Low Brass Player's Guide to Doubling

very loud indeed. Should you go this route, it will initially be much more intuitive to learn than the F contra, for obvious reasons. However, with the proliferation of quality F contras in recent years and the superior tonal characteristics of those instruments, the BB-flat is becoming increasingly rare.

Mastering New Positions

Learning a new instrument in a different key presents a number of challenges and can take significant effort. Remember that the F contra feels different, blows different, and looks different simply because it *is* different, but for a good reason. Be patient; you might need to practice the instrument for months or longer before finding the right sound. When you do, however, you will hear the sonic glory of the contrabass trombone, first on a few notes here and there, and then throughout the range of the instrument. To expedite your learning of this new instrument, you should begin with a piece of music that is:

1. Common to bass trombone

2. In a home key to the new instrument (F)

3. Not overly technical

4. Generally triadic

This is why I think the best choice for the beginning contrabass trombone player is etude #11 from the Bordogni/Wesley Jacobs - *Complete Vocalises for Tuba* (see figure 10.2). Playing only the first line or two allows the player to clearly establish the fundamental (F) in first position without the valve, then A in fourth, followed by G in first with the C attachment engaged (assuming an F/C/D-flat/AA configuration).

These are very important notes for the contrabass trombone. Play through this passage repeatedly and very slowly, all the while trying to establish as natural a sound as possible with just as much fluidity as on the bass trombone. Once the first couple of lines sound okay, take it down one octave: pedal F in first position, A in AA1 and G in AA3, etc. (This will quickly reinforce why you bought the instrument in the first place.) Try to let the vibrating portion of your lips fall into the mouthpiece and to create as resonant a sound as possible. Remember that you want to sound as good as possible as soon as possible. This will give you the intrinsic motivation to proceed, practice, and improve. Spend much time playing in these two octaves, all the while trying to produce a rich, dense, resonant

Figure 10.2: Excerpt from etude #11 from "Complete Vocalises for Tuba" by Marco Bordogni edited by Wesley Jacobs

sound. At first, some notes will sound spectacular and others will sound terrible. Just try to get them all to sound full and resonant and play as naturally as possible without overworking.

Once you have achieved proficiency, proceed with the rest of the etude as written, but always include interludes that descend to the extreme low register. Do this one etude for a week, gradually adding other materials, especially if you have music that you will need to perform on this new instrument in short order. There is no shame in writing in positions here and there as you are still becoming acclimated to the new instrument—your brain will attempt to correct your "wrong" position choice now and then, so it is better to have the correct position marked just in case. Visual reminders are essential until things become second nature.

Another thing to remember is that most F contras have only six positions with no valves engaged, and those are much longer than on the tenor or bass trombone (similar to the positions with the F attachment engaged on the tenor or bass trombones). A seventh position, when it is present at all, cannot be reached without an extension handle on the slide. The double valve system makes this unnecessary. As with the tenor and bass trombones, the number of available positions shrinks when valves are engaged. When one valve is engaged there are (at most) five reachable positions, and with both valves only four. Regular use of a tuner and/or tuning drones will be necessary to find the precise location of each position.

Choosing a Mouthpiece

When you purchase a contrabass trombone, there may or may not be a mouthpiece included. If there is, by all means use it, if for no other reason than to establish a basis for comparing other mouthpiece choices as you gain familiarity and experience with the instrument. Remember that your primary concern as a beginning contra doubler is to learn *how* to play the instrument. You will need to develop facility and feel somewhat comfortable on the instrument before you will be able to make intelligent decisions about what mouthpiece to use or any other equipment changes or enhancements to implement.

When you are ready to experiment with mouthpieces, remember that the primary consideration in choosing a contra mouthpiece (or one for any instrument) is to choose one that will allow you to play in tune in the normal playing range of the instrument. For contra, the normal playing range is outlined in figure 10.3. Above this, I have found that the tone begins to lose focus, clarity, and color.

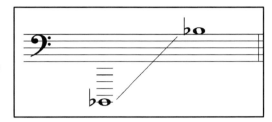

Figure 10.3: Contrabass trombone normal playing range

While the steadily growing contrabass solo literature explores greater extremes of range, generally speaking, if you are playing contra you are playing something low and/or written by a composer who desires the timbre of the contra.

Certain players will feel most comfortable with a more bowl-shaped bass trombone-style mouthpiece, while others will prefer a small tuba-style mouthpiece that is more funnel-shaped. This instrument can be played successfully with either; the best choice depends upon your sound concept and the primary instrument from which you are doubling.

Pitfalls to Avoid

Here are four common pitfalls in adding contrabass trombone to your musical life:

1. Forgetting that the contrabass trombone is a musical instrument, not a sound effect. Always endeavor to play the contra musically. Admittedly, the instrument is capable of pretty amazing sounds—ones that add drama and punctuation. At times you will feel that the music, if written specifically for contra, is not challenging. Think of this as an opportunity to let the timbre of the instrument work its magic on the ensemble.

2. Not playing the instrument enough to "get over the hump." It is easy to get discouraged initially because the contra "doesn't feel right." After about a week of playing daily, things will really begin

The Low Brass Player's Guide to Doubling

to make sense to you. It is critical that you ignore the initial discouragement. (This advice applies to taking up any secondary instrument.)

3. Actively playing the exact same music on both bass and contrabass trombones. While music that is familiar from your bass trombone studies will make the best initial practice material for contra, do try to work on separate sets of music on the two instruments. This will minimize confusion.

4. Not using a trombone stand. The contrabass trombone is exceptionally large, and leaving it on a chair or on a piano will guarantee that the instrument will be damaged. Get the most heavy-duty stand you can find for use during professional engagements *and* in your home practice space. Besides, if the instrument is left on a stand, you will be more likely to keep practicing it diligently once the novelty wears off.

Contrabass Trombone Targeted Fundamentals

Whatever routine one would use for bass trombone doubling should be transposed for contra. The Targeted Fundamentals in Appendix H have essentially the same exercises as those presented for bass trombone doublers in Appendix C, but adjusted for use on contrabass trombone. Remington-type warm-up exercises including long tones, tonguing, and lip slurs are most helpful, as is practicing scales and arpeggios. You will immediately notice that the bell is much further away and a little wider on the contra than on the bass trombone. Because of this, articulations and lip slur transitions can sound veiled or distant. For this reason, recording oneself is always a good idea, as is playing against a sonically reflective surface.

Suggested Practice and Performance Literature

As mentioned above, the Bordogni or similar etudes are a must for anyone trying to play this new instrument in a musical fashion. Pick ones you might not have played on bass and make them your "contra only" etudes. Using the tuba edition, play the etudes as written and also down one octave. Unless you are practicing contra-specific solos, this is the tessitura where you will be playing. Any of the standard bass trombone and tuba methods can provide additional practice material—a number of these are listed in Chapters 2, 6, and 8. As was mentioned previously, always use a tuner when practicing the contra; besides the need for further embouchure development in the low register, the unfamiliar positions as well as perceived spatial anomalies due to the size of the instrument can cause difficulty with finding positions and playing them in tune. The tuner can help to alleviate these difficulties.

A new resource on all things contrabass trombone is a book by Javier Colomer and Heinrich Thein entitled *The World of the Contrabass Trombone*. It provides additional perspective on the subject and contains quite a few exercises for beginning and experienced players which can be incorporated into a standard warm-up and maintenance routine.

Concluding Thoughts

If you are going to pursue contrabass trombone doubling, do so with the determination that the instrument is not a novelty. Rather, it is rather a noble and glorious instrument designed to produce a gorgeous, resonant sound. As with all instruments, the production of this sound requires diligent effort—one does not simply "pick up" the contrabass trombone. It is a unique instrument and one whose pedagogy has yet to be fully developed. It can, however, be competently learned through the re-visitation of the standard bass trombone literature and through the application of those things all brass players hold dear, especially the cultivation of a beautiful, singing approach to everything we play.

Appendix H: Contrabass Trombone Resources

Targeted Fundamentals 189

Fingering Charts 195

Overtone Series Charts 199

Chapter 11: Bass Trumpet

Brian French

Perhaps the rarest of doubling instruments in the orchestra, the bass trumpet has a narrow but important role in the repertoire. In modern symphony and opera orchestras, a trombonist is usually given the duty of performing on bass trumpet when required by the score, and these rare opportunities require careful attention and preparation.

Developed in the early nineteenth century and used almost exclusively in Central and Eastern European military bands, the bass trumpet found main-stage stardom as a prominent solo instrument in the *Ring Cycle* by Wagner. These works remain the most important excerpts in the literature; the "sword" motif, first stated midway through Act I of *Die Walküre*, is one of the most memorable of all bass trumpet excerpts, and thanks to Bugs Bunny and Elmer Fudd, is hummable by almost everyone—whether they realize it's a bass trumpet or not (see figure 11.1).

Figure 11.1: "Sword" motif from Die Walküre

Since Wagner, the bass trumpet has been used by Strauss (in some of the operas, most notably *Elektra*), Schoenberg (*Gürrelieder*), Stravinsky (*The Rite of Spring*), Janáček (*Sinfonietta, Violin Concerto*), and toward the end of the twentieth century, Henze (*Requiem*), Reimann (*Troades*), Takemitsu (*Visions*), and Ligeti, whose *La Grand Macabre* features a solo for the bass trumpeter intended to be performed from a podium in front of the orchestra.

This is a narrow repertoire indeed, and opportunities to perform most of these works are rare. All of these works are incredibly challenging for the entire orchestra, not to mention the bass trumpet parts alone; given the time constraints of the standard professional orchestral work week, it is difficult for most ensembles to prepare and perform these pieces well.

Many bass trumpeters gain their first experience on the instrument in college, where musician labor is free, music rental and production costs are minimal, and rehearsal time is abundant. Stravinsky's *Rite of Spring* and Janáček's *Sinfonietta* are both approachable by good college orchestras. The bass trumpet parts to these two works in particular are exposed but are not terribly difficult, and offer the student a challenging opportunity on a new instrument without becoming demoralized by long passages of fast fingerings and foreign transpositions.

Figure 11.2: Stravinsky's Rite of Spring features this entrance for the bass trumpet as the bottom voice of a trumpet soli.

Figure 11.3: Another excerpt from Stravinsky's Rite, this time an exposed solo entrance shared with the English horn.

While the two passages above may look demanding on first glance to players new to the valved instrument world, the passage in Figure 11.2 is very slow and encompasses only four different notes. The solo passage in Figure 11.3 is slightly more challenging but is only a short chromatic scale, and as long as the player subdivides the rests prior to the entrances, success is assured. I will discuss developing technical facility later in the chapter.

Sound Concept and Equipment

Regardless of differences in seating configuration from one orchestra to another, remember that the bass trumpet is a member of the trumpet family and should sound like a trumpet rather than a valve trombone. One should think in terms of lightness, brightness (even in the lower registers), and projection rather than the customary low brass concepts of darkness, roundness, and transparency. These are general qualities, of course; the passages at hand will dictate additional sound qualities

The Low Brass Player's Guide to Doubling

such as temperature (warmth/coldness), scope (breadth/narrowness), and shapes of articulation. Wagner, Stravinsky, Schoenberg, and Mahler were very adept at indicating exactly what they intended in their scores. Follow their markings carefully.

With these concepts in mind, note the physical characteristics of the bass trumpet as compared to that of the trombone:

- The bore of the bass trumpet is quite narrow—smaller than a jazz tenor, closer to that of an alto trombone.
- The back pressure of a bass trumpet compared to a large-bore tenor trombone is noticeable and will likely take the first-time player by surprise.
- The bell of the instrument is smaller than that of an alto trombone, usually with a slighter degree of bell flare, which affords a more projective sound.
- There are valves. But do not be intimidated; there are plenty of slides, too.

Yes, of course there are valves. In fact, just as one may see on B-flat, C, and piccolo trumpets, the bass trumpeter has a choice of piston or rotary valves—and among the rotary valve instruments, a choice of three or four valves. If money were no object, it would be optimal to have one of each: piston instruments are well suited to the Russian, French, and Czech repertoires, while rotary instruments are better suited to the Germanic repertoire.

These instruments can be expensive, however. Fortunately, student players may have access to a school-owned instrument, or may be able to procure one from a teacher or (in larger metropolitan areas) another local professional. Professionals who do not own an instrument can borrow from a trusted colleague or request that their orchestra rent a bass trumpet from a larger company, as is often done with Wagner tuben. Some world-class orchestras and opera companies own bass trumpets.

Piston valve instruments made by American manufacturers such as Bach and Kanstul tend to be less expensive (as of this writing, as much as 50% less) than rotary valve instruments made by boutique manufacturers in Germany such as Alexander, Thein, Scherzer, and Schagerl. Within the "value-priced" category, the instrument available from the Czech manufacturer Červený approaches consistent playability. Occasionally one may find a good used instrument online from a reputable manufacturer, but avoid the "professional hand-made" brass instruments from low quality Asian

The Low Brass Player's Guide to Doubling

manufacturers with Germanic brand names sold very cheaply on online auction sites. Even high quality bass trumpets have their playing challenges; low-end instruments exacerbate these challenges exponentially.

The available keys of these instruments are something to consider. In the United States, the most popular choice is the B-flat instrument, with the same sounding pitch as the trombone or euphonium, one octave lower than the B-flat trumpet. In Europe, C instruments are more widely played, although some opera houses own the higher E-flat instruments. Bass trumpets in F and D, although they exist, are very rare. It may be a matter of personal preference, but many players find the B-flat instruments lend themselves to easier transpositions. It may also be easier to conceptualize in one's mind that first position on a trombone and open valves on a B-flat bass trumpet will produce the same sounding pitches (as will second position and second valve, third position and first valve, and so on). Those who already play euphonium might find B-flat instruments to be especially to their liking, since the euphonium and B-flat bass trumpet have identical fingering systems (certain low register fingerings on compensating euphoniums excepted).

All bass trumpets present something of an intonational game of chance, and players will find that constant adjustments must be made. As has been mentioned repeatedly in this book, familiarity with the overtone series chart and the usual tendencies of each partial for the instrument you are playing can aid you in anticipating and effecting needed adjustments, whether with the embouchure, by moving slides, or by choosing alternate fingerings. The availability of a fourth valve can also help relieve the burden on the embouchure as a means of pitch adjustment. The fourth valve works much in the same way as a trombone's F-attachment and in exactly the same way as the fourth valve on a non-compensating euphonium, lowering the pitch of the instrument by a perfect fourth while allowing for a wider choice of alternate fingerings. Three-valve instruments at the very least should have working first- and third-valve slides, and players may consider having mechanisms for extending the main tuning slide (operated by the right thumb) mounted to their instruments by a custom technician. For more information on fourth valves and main tuning slide triggers, see the discussion of similar equipment for the euphonium in Chapter 5.

Mouthpiece choice is an important consideration for the bass trumpet. Bearing in mind that the sound should be more like that of a trumpet than a trombone, look for a mouthpiece with a shallower cup, a medium throat, and a slightly smaller backbore for a more brilliant sound, while maintaining a reasonable similarity to the rim size and cup diameter of your primary instrument's mouthpiece. This may necessitate a custom build. Players who perform on alto trombone may find that the same mouthpiece works well for both instruments, although some may prefer an even shallower cup size for bass trumpet.

Holding Position

As there are two different kinds of bass trumpets—piston and rotary—there are two very different holding positions.

The piston-valved bass trumpet should be held just as a regular piston trumpet is held: the left hand wraps around the valve casing with the left thumb and ring finger manipulating the first- and third-valve tuning slides. The right thumb supports from underneath the leadpipe, with the right pinky usually in a support soldered to the end of the leadpipe just before the first bow. As mentioned above, some piston trumpets may have a main tuning slide throw operated by the

Figure 11.4: Correct holding position for a piston valve bass trumpet

Figure 11.5: Correct holding position for a rotary valve bass trumpet

right thumb or pinky finger (see figure 11.4).

Holding a rotary-valved bass trumpet can feel quite unnatural at first. Because of the added weight of the valves—especially if there are four—these instruments are heavier than their piston counterparts, and differences in bracing from manufacturer to manufacturer can make it difficult to find a natural holding position; however, the benefits in sound quality can outweigh this initial awkwardness. The left thumb should offer most of the support, resting under a brace, while two or three left fingers rest on the bell; the left pinky (or ring finger and pinky) support from under the bell. The right thumb also supports from underneath, resting under a brace, and on a three-valve instrument, the pinky rests underneath or against the tubing nearest to the valve buttons (see figure 11.5).

Maintenance and Technical Facility

As discussed earlier in this book, you should regularly practice Targeted Fundamentals to maintain and develop both good sound and good technique on a doubling instrument. It is also advised that daily maintenance on the primary instrument be carried out first whenever possible, to facilitate the transference of good playing habits from the primary instrument to the bass trumpet.

A couple of minutes of buzzing on the smaller bass trumpet mouthpiece, followed by long tones and very slow lip slurs at the beginning of a practice day, are very important exercises not only to cultivate a core sound but also to acclimate to the inherent stuffiness of the bass trumpet as compared to the free-blowing feel of a trombone. Reap the rewards from a patient ten minutes of long tones on this instrument—your embouchure and breathing apparatus will thank you for it. Just as one would practice on the trombone, long tones should also be played in various dynamics. It is particularly more difficult to play forte and fortissimo with a stable tone in the lower register of the bass trumpet, given the greater resistance as compared to the trombone.

This period of long-tone work is also a good time to focus on pitch and intervals. Listen to yourself. Do you need to lip down that descending minor second? Do you need to blow through that ascending major sixth to find the bottom of the arrival pitch? Become acquainted with your left thumb and ring finger—the ones that operate the 1st- and 3rd-valve slides. Long tone practice is the perfect time to accomplish this.

Scales—particularly chromatic scales—are effective means of developing a number of different performance mechanisms: pitch, rhythm, focus, relaxation, articulation, evenness of tone, and finger dexterity, a relatively foreign concept for trombonists. The distance one finger travels to push down an open valve does not even begin to compare with the distance that a trombonist's right hand travels from first position to fifth, sixth, or seventh. Relax. Benefit from slow and considered practice, and finger dexterity will happen. One of the most effective exercises is a simple half-octave chromatic scale passage in the middle register (see figure 11.6).

Figure 11.6: Brief, half-octave chromatic exercises such as this develop finger dexterity and a relaxed breath.

Played daily in several different keys, this easy exercise works wonders to develop fingering technique as well as efficient blowing, relaxation, and a big orchestral trumpet sound. Besides this, the Targeted Fundamentals presented in Appendix I provides an opportunity to review and extend your bass trumpet playing skills in a concise but thorough manner.

Performing on the bass trumpet requires a healthy three octave range, so a regimen of scales and arpeggios encompassing and extending a sizable range should be practiced regularly. Wagner's "rainbow" motif at the end of *Das Rheingold* presents nearly all three octaves at once, rising over the course of sixteen measures from a concert D-flat below the treble clef staff to concert high F and back again, ending on a very strong (and hopefully very stable) low D-flat (see figure 11.7).

Some passages in Schoenberg's *Gürrelieder* require a particularly strong low register, while works such as the Henze *Requiem* remain stratospherically high.

Transposition

A primary element of performing on bass trumpet is transposition, a concept unfamiliar to many trombonists. Just as passages in the trumpet and horn parts of Classical and Romantic works are often indicated "in F" or "in E-flat" or "in D," so are bass trumpet parts. The Janáček *Sinfonietta* is for B-flat bass trumpet, while Stravinsky's *Rite of Spring* is an E-flat part, as is Schoenberg's

Figure 11.7: The "Rainbow (Regenbogen)" motif from Wagner's Das Rheingold (E-flat bass trumpet)

Gürrelieder; Strauss and Wagner operas change variously between bass trumpet in E-flat, D, F, C, and B-flat.

Transposition can be a challenge, but it should not be a deterrent. One simply needs to understand that there is a distinction between *written* notes and *sounding* or *concert* pitches. Bass trumpet parts are written in treble clef, with C bass trumpet parts sounding an octave lower than written, B-flat parts sounding a major ninth lower than written, E-flat bass trumpet parts a major sixth lower than written, D bass trumpet parts a minor seventh lower than written, and F bass trumpet parts a perfect fifth lower than written.

There are two basic methods to the practice of transposition. When transposing by **interval**, the performer determines the interval between the written key and the key of the instrument, and simply reads (imagines) the written passage up or down according to that interval. In other words, a performer with a B-flat bass trumpet playing the *Rite of Spring,* an E-flat bass trumpet part, would read the part as if it were a perfect fourth higher. Someone with a C bass trumpet playing the B-flat part to Janáček's *Sinfonietta* or his *Violin Concerto* would imagine the part down a major second.

Transposing by **clef** may be the easiest concept to apply, because trombonists are required to read bass, tenor, and alto clefs on a regular basis anyway. A musician playing the *Rite of Spring* would imagine the written E-flat treble clef part as if it were in bass clef, adding three flats to the key

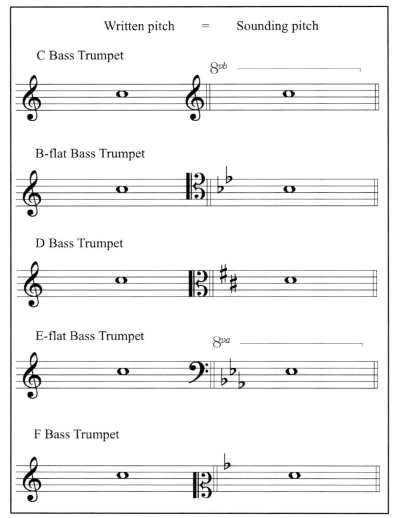

Figure 11.8: Using clefs to read bass trumpet parts

signature and playing up an octave. The same musician playing the B-flat Janáček would read the treble clef part as if it were in tenor clef, adding two flats to the key signature. Clefs can be used to read the most common transpositions for bass trumpet parts (see figure 11.8).

Suggested Practice and Performance Literature

As a specialty instrument used primarily in large symphonic and operatic works, the bass trumpet lacks solo repertoire and has few dedicated study materials. Still, the use of bass trumpet-specific resources, along with the appropriation of trumpet methods, can aid in the development of a correct sound concept, informed interpretation of bass trumpet excerpts, and necessary technical proficiency. The Shifrin/Hanlon excerpts volume is indispensable, covering the above mentioned standard works as well as additional pieces in which conductors might request bass trumpet even though it is not expressly called for in the score. Another invaluable resource is Michael Mulcahy's recording of the Wagner Ring passages on his recording of orchestral excerpts. Mulcahy's masterful playing not only provides insight on the performance approach to these operas, but sets a gold-standard concept of sound to which all bass trumpeters should aspire. The traditional trumpet methods listed here can be employed both for improving technical proficiency and for transposition practice as needed.

Arban, Jean-Baptiste, edited by Allen Vizzutti - *Complete Method for Trumpet*

Bitsch, Marcel - *20 Etudes for Trumpet*

Bordogni, Marco, edited by Larry Clark and Sean O'Loughlin - *Melodious Etudes for Trumpet*

Caffarelli, Reginaldo - *100 Melodic Studies in Transposition*

Charlier, Theophilus - *36 études transcendantes*

Clarke, Herbert L. - *Technical Studies for the Cornet*

Reynolds, Jeffrey and Michael Mulcahy - *Orchestral Excerpts for Bass Trombone, Tenor Tuba, Bass Trumpet* (compact disc recording)

Saint-Jacome, Louis A. - *Grand Method for Trumpet or Cornet*

Schlossberg, Max - *Daily Drills and Technical Studies for Trumpet*

Shifrin, Ken, edited by Ken Hanlon - *The Professional's Handbook of Orchestral Excerpts for Euphonium and Bass Trumpet*

Vacchiano, William - *Moving Transposition (after Ernst Sachse's 100 Etudes for Trumpet)*

Vizzutti, Allen - *The Allen Vizzutti Trumpet Method* (3 volumes)

Appendix I: Bass Trumpet Resources

Targeted Fundamentals.. 201

Fingering Charts... 207

Overtone Series Charts... 211

Chapter 12: Cimbasso

J. Mark Thompson

Introduction

The cimbasso belongs to the trombone family, in spite of the fact that it uses valves instead of a traditional trombone slide to manipulate the tubing length. It is usually pitched in F or BB-flat (although versions in E-flat and CC exist) and has three to six piston or rotary valves. The cimbasso's predominantly cylindrical bore gives it a wide ranging tone quality, from warm and mellow to bright and menacing. It plays in the same range as a tuba or contrabass trombone and is thus usually played by a tuba or bass trombone player.

Though its use began in the opera pit, the cimbasso has found its way onto the concert stage and into jazz, commercial, and solo settings. While there are many incarnations of the cimbasso, this chapter will refer to the most common instrument pitched in F.

History

The original cimbasso was a member of the upright serpent or bass horn family. It was invented about 1815, and Paganini called for it in his *Violin Concerto No. 1*. This instrument was replaced

Figure 12.1: Correct cimbasso playing position

The Low Brass Player's Guide to Doubling

by, in rapid succession, the keyed ophicleide, valved ophicleide, bombardon, serpentone, and pelittone, all of which have roughly the same pitch range. While there was much change in the available instruments, the terms used to describe them did not change as rapidly and tended to become a regional practice. Also, there was great inconsistency in the publishing of scores, with the composers and copyists frequently changing terms within the same work (from *The Tuba Family* by Clifford Bevan).

By 1871, it became standard to use a valved bass trombone in F as the lowest member of the low brass section in Italian orchestras. In that year, Verdi served as president of a committee tasked with the reform of the conservatories, which recommended the use of four trombones and no other low brass in large orchestras. Verdi included the new valved contrabass trombone in BB-flat for his last two operas, *Otello* and *Falstaff*, and the combination of two tenor trombones in B-flat, bass trombone in F and contrabass trombone in BB-flat was used by Puccini in all his operas except *Manon Lescaut*. This section became solidified in late Romantic Italian works until 1934.

After the introduction of the BB-flat valved contrabass trombone, it became common practice to apply this instrument retroactively to earlier works. Eventually, a bass-contrabass trombone was built that was pitched in F with a slide and two independent valves in C and D (together BB-flat) that would be suitable in tone concept to cover these parts, yet not quite so unwieldy as the contrabass models. This instrument was called a "cimbasso contrabass trombone," and thus began the development of the modern contrabass trombone (see Chapter 10).

Valved models of these instruments are in increasing use today, and there are many models available in four-, five-, and six-valve versions pitched in F, or generally four-valved models pitched in BB-flat. These instruments are all in the family of the valved contrabass trombone—the modern cimbasso.

Sound Concept and Blending

The most compelling reason to play a cimbasso is to produce an authentic tone spectrum capable of blending with the other cylindrical brasses. Using a section of trombones and cimbasso fully completes the cylindrical brass from soprano (trumpet) through contrabass (cimbasso). A second reason is that the sound of the cimbasso is directed forward like the trombones rather than upward like the tuba, which blends less well in the orchestra pit, especially when seated under the overhang of the stage. Simply put, the cimbasso helps the section blend and helps get the sound out of the pit.

The Low Brass Player's Guide to Doubling

Verdi was very specific in defining the sound concept of the low brass section. As such, the principal concern of any performer of the cimbasso is to match the sound as closely as possible to the bass trombone or the contrabass trombone in F. A bass trombonist doubling on cimbasso will have a distinct advantage in this regard, since this tone concept is ingrained into the bass trombonist's everyday playing. Tuba players who double regularly on bass trombone, even if only in jazz and commercial settings, will also have an excellent tone concept to match. However, for tuba players who play bass and contrabass tubas exclusively, this tone concept can prove elusive. Spending some time on a bass trombone, if only to build rudimentary skills, can yield excellent results in developing a proper sound concept on cimbasso. For all players, access to a slide contrabass trombone, discussed in Chapter 10, would be a distinct advantage in cultivating the proper sound concept.

Choosing an Instrument

Recent interest in the cimbasso has drawn the attention of many major instrument makers. Notable manufacturers include, but are not limited to: Gebr. Alexander, Thein Brass, Musik Haag AG, Červený, Mirafone, G&P Wind Instruments (formerly Kalison), Lätzsch Custom Brass, Meinl-Weston, Rudolf Meinl, and Voight Brass.

The majority of cimbassi are constructed in F with at least four valves. I prefer a five-valve F cimbasso, as this configuration yields a fully chromatic instrument that includes the low G-flat that is missing on a three- or four-valve model. There are many valve configurations and types available on cimbassi. Most common are models pitched in F that utilize four or five valves. Six-valve models come at additional expense, but may be preferred if the instrument is in regular use. Three-valve models also exist; however, their use would be limited to works prior to Verdi's *Otello* and *Falstaff* and most of Puccini's works, because notes from B-flat down to G-flat are not available on the three-valve instrument.

Rotary valve models are most common, although G&P Wind Instruments (formerly Kalison) makes piston valve models in F and BB-flat and an F model with four piston valves and a rotary fifth valve. Thein Brass and Musik Haag AG have models equipped with Hagmann valves.

Bore sizes vary considerably, and special consideration must be given to this specification in order to achieve the proper tone and character. When properly matched with a mouthpiece, the general sound should be that of a bass trombone, not a tuba. Instrument manufacturers are developing cimbasso models with increasingly larger bore sizes—instruments that start in larger bore sizes and those whose bores increase in size throughout the instrument. Both approaches—especially the latter—carry the sound concept out of the realm of the cylindrical trombone-family sound into the realm of the conical tuba-family sound. I prefer cimbassi of medium-large bore to properly convey Verdi's preferred sound concept.

Holding Position

Adjust the peg so the mouthpiece meets your embouchure comfortably—as with all the other instruments, bring the instrument to you, not the other way around (see figure 12.1). The fingers of the right hand should be positioned on the end of each valve paddle, and the right thumb may rest underneath the second valve ring or behind the lead pipe tubing (see figure 12.2). The fingers of the left hand should grip the bent curve of the instrument so the left thumb can touch the fifth valve paddle.

Figure 12.2: Cimbasso hand positions

The Low Brass Player's Guide to Doubling

Mastering Fingerings

It is unlikely that someone who is asked to play cimbasso would not have some form of previous valve experience. Basic scale patterns, various exercises (Remington, Clarke, Schlossberg, Arban), and working the specific passages in question are the most immediate methods to build security and confidence. Chromatic passages and scalewise technique abound in these books, as well as arpeggiated sequences. The Targeted Fundamentals presented in Appendix F can be used on both tuba and cimbasso; in addition, the scale and arpeggio routines in Appendix B are useful materials for skill development and maintenance. Perhaps not so surprisingly, there are not many method books about the cimbasso. Still, there are a few that have good basic information and even some exercises and etudes (Bianchini, Mariani, Colomer & Thein).

Choosing a Mouthpiece

Selecting a proper mouthpiece for cimbasso can be a difficult task. Most cimbassi come with a tuba shank receiver, but the size and proportions of the mouthpiece must favor those of a large bass trombone or even a contrabass trombone mouthpiece. That is, a predominantly deep, cup-shaped mouthpiece, rather than a more traditional funnel-shaped mouthpiece. The key is to keep the sound of the cylindrical brass family and not the conical family. A few manufacturers include contrabass trombone mouthpieces in their catalogs, but some models may not be available with a tuba shank. It is possible to have a custom mouthpiece made or to assemble a modular mouthpiece to specifications that include a tuba shank.

Pitfalls to Avoid

1. Improper sound concept.

Trying to sound like a small-bore tuba or even euphonium does not achieve a homogeneous trombone section sound. This is not the time to channel your "inner tuba." The sound must fit securely as an extension of the trombone sound concept into the bass and contrabass registers. Playing passages on a bass trombone (or a contrabass trombone, if one is available) then playing them again on the cimbasso is a great way to match the sound concept. Record both, compare, note what differences there are and adjust, then repeat the process. You should seek to cultivate the most natural sound possible. If you can arrange the opportunity, have others listen to you while you are

The Low Brass Player's Guide to Doubling

playing in the pit. Encourage and accept any advice that is given.

2. *Failing to practice music characteristic to the cimbasso.*

Music written for the cimbasso fits historically into the approximately one hundred year period from 1829-1934, almost exclusively in Romantic Italian operas. It is wise to become more than familiar with these works (please refer to the list at the end of this chapter), since this body of music will be your greatest opportunity to perform on the cimbasso.

3. *Poor intonation.*

Begin your development by playing music with which you are already familiar. This will help you isolate areas of the instrument that are not responsive or highlight notes that are out of tune. For bass trombonists, there is no handslide to make minor adjustments in pitch; this must be fine tuned with the embouchure, wind, and possibly tuning slide adjustments if time permits. For tubists, the idiosyncrasies found in the cimbasso might be predictably similar to those of an F tuba; however, the cimbasso is more cylindrical, and it may not exhibit the exact tendencies of your bass tuba. After you have achieved some success in playing standard etude literature, begin recording yourself to help further refine your cimbasso ear.

4. *Thinking "in B-flat."*

The cimbasso is a bass-contrabass instrument in F. While there are many characteristics that are similar to those of the bass trombone, it is essential to understand the harmonic series so that you will know how to "find yourself" on the cimbasso. Those who already play F tuba will have little difficulty with this; those approaching the cimbasso from trombone or euphonium will find it more challenging. Some fingerings will be the same as some partials on a euphonium, bass trumpet, or valve trombone; notably, the fourth and eighth partial fingerings of the cimbasso match the third and sixth partial fingerings on the B-flat valved instruments, respectively, but little else does. Learn the fingerings and why they work.

5. *Failure to maintain wind column efficiency.*

As you are developing your skill set for the cimbasso, don't forget to keep the wind moving efficiently as you play. The wind column is the key to proper tone production, projection,

120

The Low Brass Player's Guide to Doubling

intonation, and section balance.

6. *Not studying the full score.*

This will go a long way in telling you how your sound should fit into the texture. While there are many times you are playing with the trombone section, there are other times that you are assisting the horn section (also pitched in F) and yet still other times when you are reinforcing the bass line with the double basses, cellos, and bassoons. Sometimes your voice must blend perfectly and other times it should lead. Studying the score in advance can give you a pretty clear picture of the function of the cimbasso in the texture.

Suggested Practice and Performance Literature

These materials provide sufficient variety to yield a rounded practice regimen. Regular practice of scales and arpeggios is invaluable in developing the necessary technique for cimbasso. In addition to the scale and arpeggio routine provided in Appendix B, SmartMusic (a subscription-based software program available at www.smartmusic.com) is an excellent tool for scales, apreggios, and additional exercises.

Tempos in opera productions can vary widely, often being conducted considerably faster than indicated in the parts. Many recordings exist that can be of great benefit in learning the particular styles, tempos, and balance of a proper low bass section in the context of a full production. The list of books and works below is not comprehensive, but it is establishes an excellent starting point to develop the basics.

Method and Etude Books

> Bordogni, Giulio Marco, edited by Allen Ostrander - *Melodious Etudes for Bass Trombone*
> Colomer, Javier, and Heinrich Thein - *The World of the Contrabass Trombone*
> Fink, Reginald H., compiler & ed. - *Studies in Legato from the works of Concone, Marchesi, and Panofka for Bass Trombone or Tuba*
> Getchell, Robert W., edited by Nilo W. Hovey - *First* and *Second Books of Practical Studies for Tuba*
> Gower, William, and Hymie Voxman - *Rubank Advanced Method for E-flat or BB-flat Bass*

The Low Brass Player's Guide to Doubling

(Vols. I & II)

Kietzer, Robert, trans. by Theodore Baker - *Schule für Tuba in F und Es oder Helikon*, Op. 84 (free download from imslp.org/wiki/Category:Kietzer,_Robert)

Kopprasch, C. *[sic]*, edited by Franz Seyffarth - *Sechzig [60] ausgewählte Etüden für Tuba (oder Helikon),* Op. 6 (Books 1 & 2)

Kopprasch, Georg, adopted for bass trombone by Benny Sluchin - *60 Études*, Op. 5 (free download from http://www.yeodoug.com/kopprasch.html)

The following items may be adapted easily by reading them in tenor clef down an octave (i.e., down a perfect fourth) or by reading them down an octave.

Bordogni, Giulio Marco, transcribed and progressively arranged by Joannes Rochut, edited by Alan Raph - *Melodious Etudes for Trombone*

Clarke, Herbert L., edited by Claude Gordon, transposed into bass clef by William B. Knevitt - *Technical Studies for Bass Clef Instruments*

Schlossberg, Max, edited by C. K. Schlossberg - *Daily Drills and Technical Studies for Trombone*

Orchestral Excerpt Books

Ferrari, Bruno - *Passi Difficili e "A Solo" per Trombone e Basso Tuba da Opera Liriche Italiane* (Books 1-4)

(at the time of publication, the valved bass trombone had fallen into disuse in Italy, and the compiler, principal trombone at La Scala, refers to the bass tuba throughout, though it is indicated by "B.T.")

Sala, Marco - *Passi d'Orchestra per Basso-Tuba su Opere di Giuseppe Verdi* (while the book includes "Basso-Tuba" in the title, each work is identified either with "Cimbasso," "Trombone Basso," or "Ophicleide," with no actual references to tuba)

The Low Brass Player's Guide to Doubling

Verdi, Giuseppe, edited by Alfred Stöneberg - *Orchester-Studien für Posaune und Basstuba* (Books 1-6) (it was an editorial choice of this German publisher to refer to the 4th trombone part as "Tuba" throughout)

Works Best Performed on the Modern Cimbasso

Operatic Works

Bellini: *La Straniera* (1829), *Norma* (1831)

Boïto: *Mefistofele* (1868)

Catalani: *Loreley* (1890), *La Wally* (1892)

Donizetti: *Parisina* (1833), *La favorite* (1840)

Puccini: *Le Villi* (1884), *Edgar* (1889), *La bohème* (1896), *Tosca* (1900), *Madama Butterfly* (1904), *La fanciulla del West* (1910), *La rondine* (1917), *Il trittico: Il tabarro* (1918), *Il trittico: Suor Angelica (1918), Il trittico: Gianni Schicchi* (1918), *Turandot* (1926)

Verdi: *Oberto* (1839), *Un giorno di regno* (1840), *Nabucodonosor (Nabucco)* (1842), *I Lombardi alla prima crociata* (1843), *I due foscari* (1844), *Ernani* (1844), *Giovanna d'Arco* (1845), *Alzira* (1845), *Attila* (1846), *Macbeth* (1847), *I masnadieri* (1847), *Jérusalem* (1847), *Il corsaro* (1848), *La battaglia di Legnano* (1849), *Luisa Miller* (1849), *Stiffelio* (1850), *Rigoletto* (1851), *Il trovatore* (1853), *La traviata* (1853), *Les vêpres siciliennes (I vespri siciliani)* (1855), *Simone Boccanegra* (1857), *Aroldo* (1857), *Un Ballo en Maschera* (1859), *La forza del destino* (1862), *Don Carlos* (1867), *Aïda* (1871), *Otello* (1887), *Falstaff* (1893)

Symphonic and Other Concert Works

Puccini: *Messa di Gloria* (1880)

Respighi: *Pini di Roma* (1924), *Belkis, Regina di Saba* (1934)

Verdi: *Messa di Requiem* (1874), *Quattro Pezzi sacri* (1897)

Appendix F: Tuba and Cimbasso Resources

Targeted Fundamentals.. 159

Fingering Charts 171

Overtone Series Charts 179

Appendix A: Daily Practice Regimens

Below are four practice schedules, beginning with a version that includes the extended work which might be undertaken by a performance major at a college or university, and ending with a shorter schedule which might be used on a day with severely limited time for practice—whether by the professional player with a heavy gig schedule or the avocational player whose responsibilities outside of music leave little time for more than daily maintenance. The longer schedules should not be performed in a single sitting, and can be divided as needed into multiple shorter sessions. All of these schedules can be modified to suit individual needs.

Any of these schedules can be used by players who play only one secondary instrument in addition to the primary instrument, as well as by those who double on several different instruments. While all these practice regimens emphasize fundamental playing skills, the shorter schedules are skewed even more in favor of fundamental exercises because the skills developed and maintained by practicing fundamental exercises apply to all of the music that you play, not just individual pieces. When practice time is lacking and you must choose between practicing fundamentals and repertoire, fundamentals should always receive top priority (except, of course, in rare occasions when you must prepare for an immediate and unexpected performance obligation). Sight reading, while important, has not been listed as a separate category; I prefer to treat that as a subset of work on performance and study materials.

I have not adjusted the suggested timings depending upon the number of secondary instruments you play. The primary instrument always receives first priority, with secondary instrument practice receiving only 20-30% of your practice time in each regimen, regardless of the number of secondary instruments you play. This reflects the importance of having a single primary instrument and is representative of the proportions of practice time I suggest you devote to primary and secondary instrument practice. While you might reason that adding additional doubling instruments should lead to a greater proportion of time devoted to secondary instrument practice, I have learned through experience that doing so leads to the "jack of all trades and master of none" phenomenon that I want to avoid, where all of the instruments are played at an equally mediocre level. Devoting the majority of your practice time to mastering a single primary instrument promotes an advanced level of musicianship that trickles down to the secondary instruments. When the materials chosen for secondary instrument practice effectively target areas of difference between the primary and secondary instruments while allowing areas of similarity to transfer between instruments, the development of high level musicianship on the primary instrument leads to similarly high level musicianship on all instruments with a minimal time commitment.

These regimens include only one Targeted Fundamentals Routine on a secondary instrument for each day's practice. Those that play multiple doubling instruments should rotate, playing the Targeted Fundamentals on a different secondary instrument each day. Scales and arpeggios are practiced on each doubling instrument each day. This schedule facilitates the regular covering of all needed fundamental playing skills on all instruments without allowing the amount of daily work to become excessive. Despite their importance, there is a limit to how much time one can spend on fundamental exercises each day! That said, when adding a new secondary instrument, the Targeted Fundamentals for that instrument should be performed daily, along with scales and arpeggios and additional time given to introductory method books. Some practice time for the new instrument can be borrowed from the time normally spent in other areas, though lengthening the practice day for work on the new instrument is preferable whenever possible. Once the new instrument is well in hand, it can assume a place in the normal rotation.

Practice Regimen #1: 3-4 Hours

5 minutes: Breathing exercises

10 minutes: Mouthpiece buzzing exercises

35-45 minutes: Daily routine, primary instrument

10-15 minutes: Secondary instrument Targeted Fundamentals

10-20 minutes: Scales and arpeggios, all instruments

50-60 minutes: Solo and chamber repertoire, primary instrument

35-45 minutes: Methods and excerpts, primary instrument

25-40 minutes: Performance and study repertoire, secondary instruments

Practice Regimen #2: 2-3 Hours

5 minutes: Breathing exercises

10 minutes: Mouthpiece buzzing exercises

35-45 minutes: Daily routine, primary instrument

10-15 minutes: Secondary instrument Targeted Fundamentals

5-10 minutes: Scales and arpeggios, all instruments

25-40 minutes: Solo and chamber repertoire, primary instrument

15-30 minutes: Methods and excerpts, primary instrument

15-25 minutes: Performance and study repertoire, secondary instruments

Practice Regimen #3: 1-2 Hours

3-5 minutes: Breathing exercises

5-10 minutes: Mouthpiece buzzing exercises

12-20 minutes: Daily routine, primary instrument

8-12 minutes: Secondary instrument Targeted Fundamentals

4-8 minutes: Scales and arpeggios, all instruments

12-25 minutes: Solo and chamber repertoire, primary instrument

8-20 minutes: Methods and excerpts, primary instrument

8-20 minutes: Performance and study repertoire, secondary instruments

Practice Regimen #4: 30-60 minutes (Maintenance only)

3-5 minutes: Breathing exercises

5-7 minutes: Mouthpiece buzzing exercises

10-18 minutes: Daily routine, primary instrument

8-10 minutes: Secondary instrument Targeted Fundamentals

4-8 minutes: Scales and arpeggios, all instruments

0-7 minutes: Performance and study repertoire, any instrument

The Low Brass Player's Guide to Doubling

Appendix B: Sample Scale Routines

On the following pages are two samples of a scale routine: high and low. Choose the appropriate version for the instrument you are working on and change the ranges and octaves as needed to accommodate your instrument and playing range. These samples are in the key of B-flat and are intended as templates for other keys; choose a different key in which to play this sequence of scales and arpeggios each day. Organizing scale and arpeggio practice by key area rather than by type of scale or arpeggio provides for daily review of the tonal relationships within each type of pattern, while conserving practice time by spreading the regular review of scale and arpeggio patterns over the course of twelve days (one day for each key). Experimenting with different articulations, dynamic levels, rhythms, and octaves can make a routine like this extremely useful and adaptable to a variety of playing situations.

The first section, diatonic pattern scales or revolving scales, moves through each of the modes, retaining the same key signature. The second section should be slightly faster than the first, and involves repetition of major and relative minor scales, arpeggios, and thirds. The repetition is mainly for the purpose of providing additional review. The third section consists of full range major and parallel minor scales, and should be played at a slower tempo, with emphasis given to playing with a full and consistent sound throughout the tonal range. The fourth section includes a number of patterns that have become increasingly common, particularly in jazz and commercial contexts. I usually only perform two-octave triad and seventh-chord arpeggios in the fifth section in order to save time, but additional octaves can be added if desired, as can ninth, eleventh, and thirteenth chords, etc. The routine ends with a chromatic scale, with the starting and ending pitches determined by the key area for each day's routine. I sometimes play this scale slowly to develop consistency of tone and tuning, while other times I play it more quickly to practice technique. There is value to both approaches.

For doubling practice, I usually divide this routine between instruments on a single day, often playing sections 1-2 on one instrument, 3-4 on another, and 5-6 on yet another instrument; you can use whatever division of labor best suits your needs. With less advanced students my usual practice is to use only sections 1, 2, and 6, with a smaller tonal range required for the chromatic scale.

128

Sample Scale and Arpeggio Practice Routine: High Version

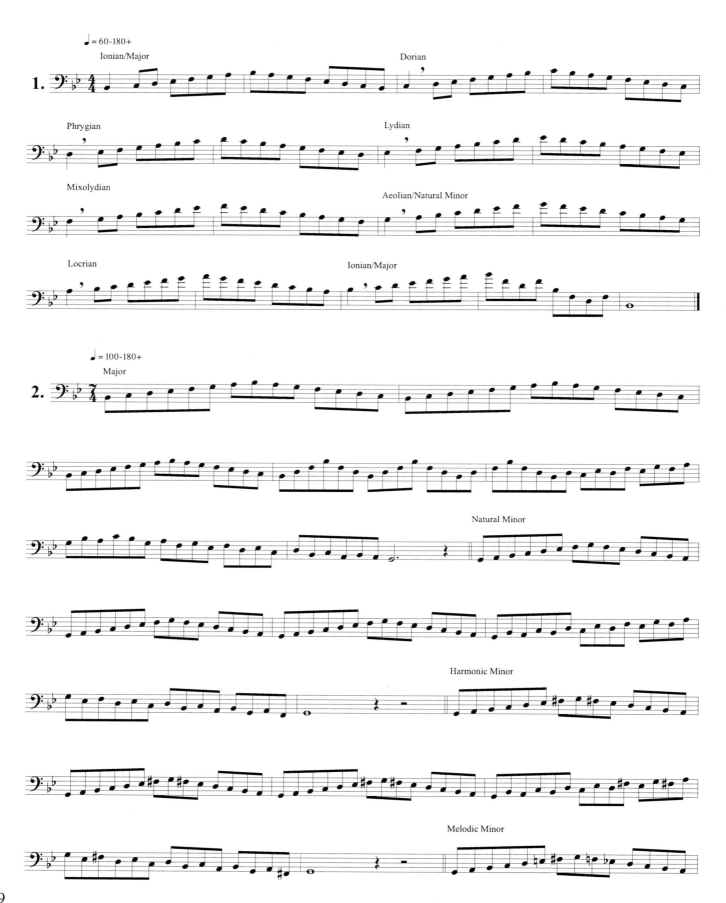

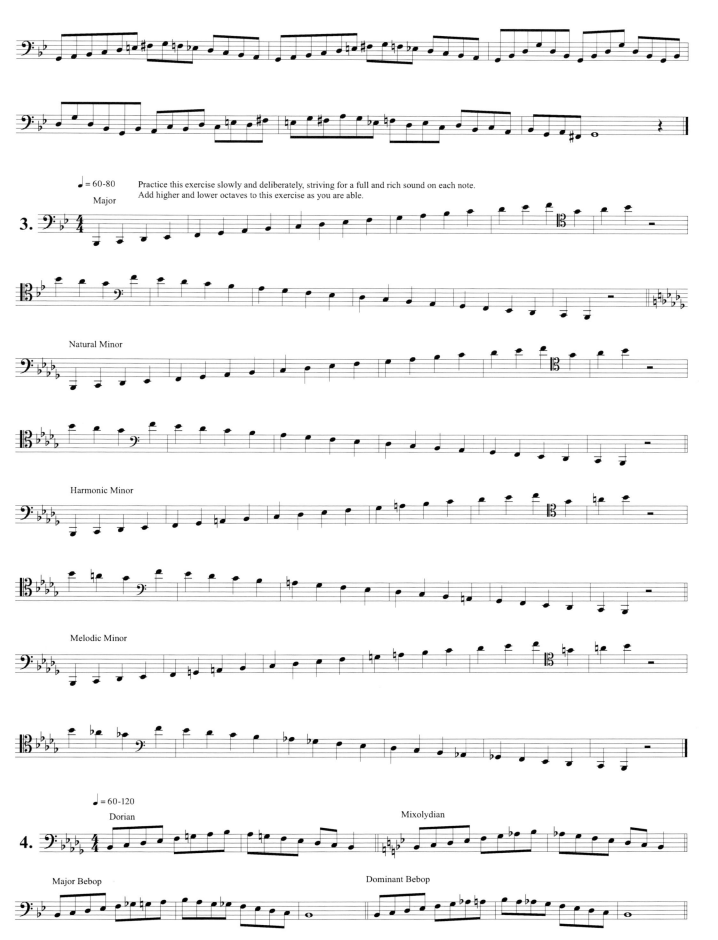

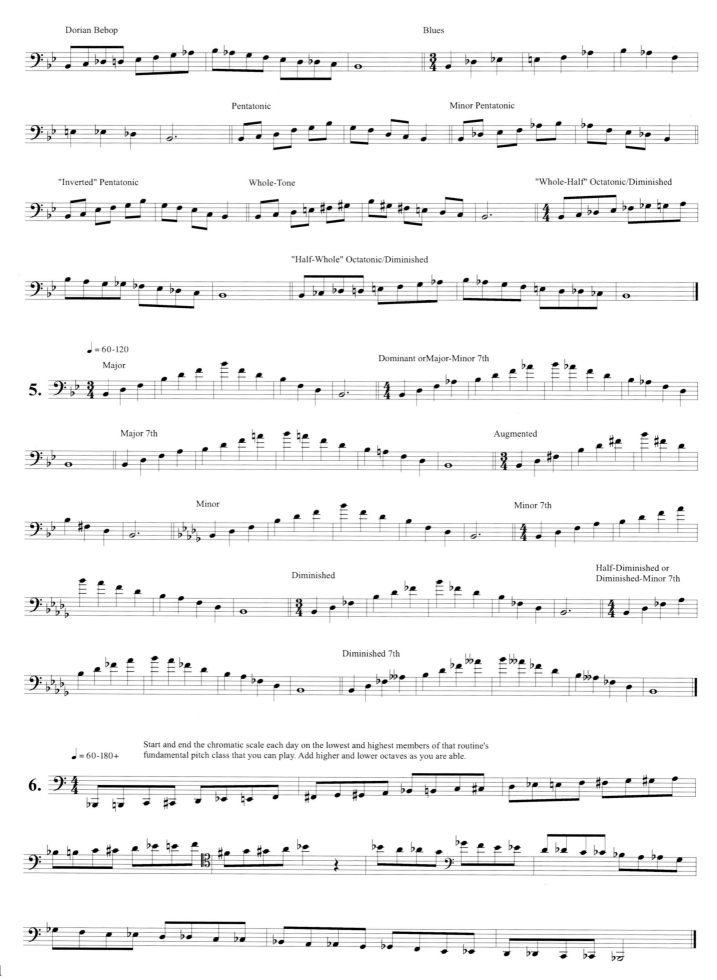

Sample Scale and Arpeggio Practice Routine: Low Version

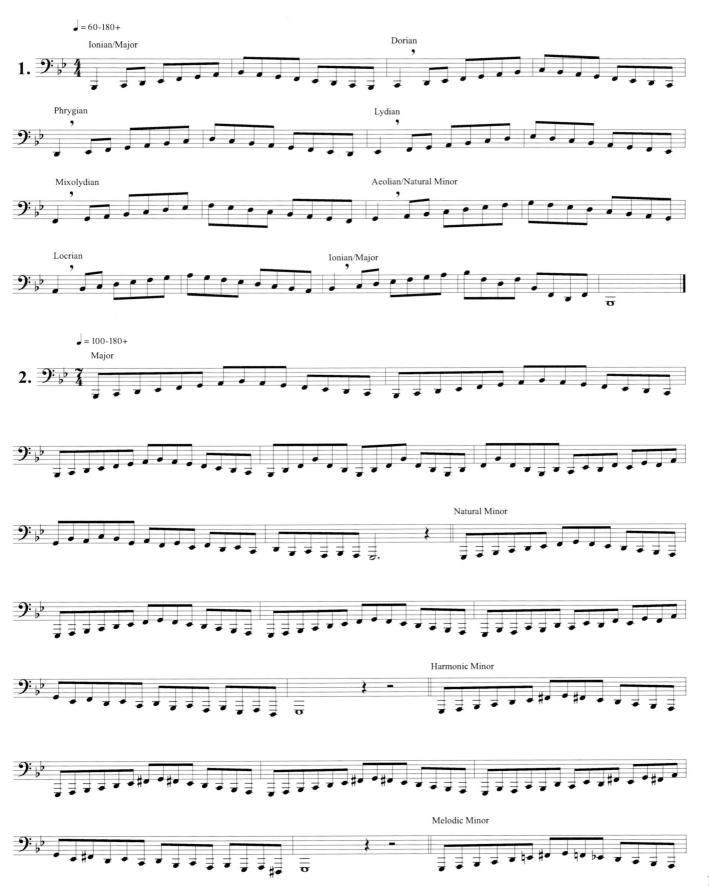

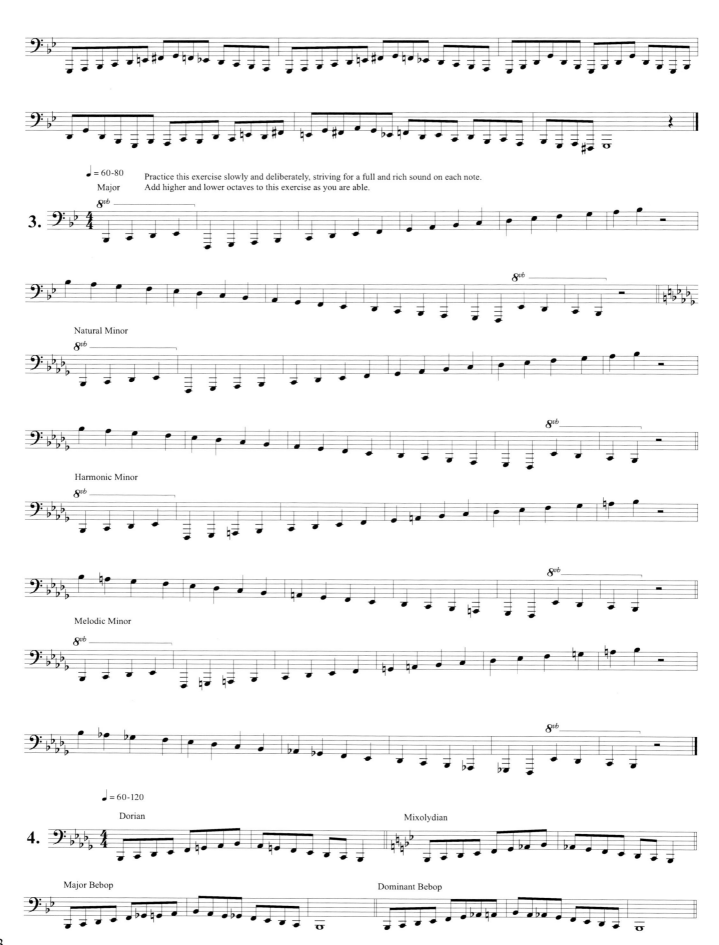

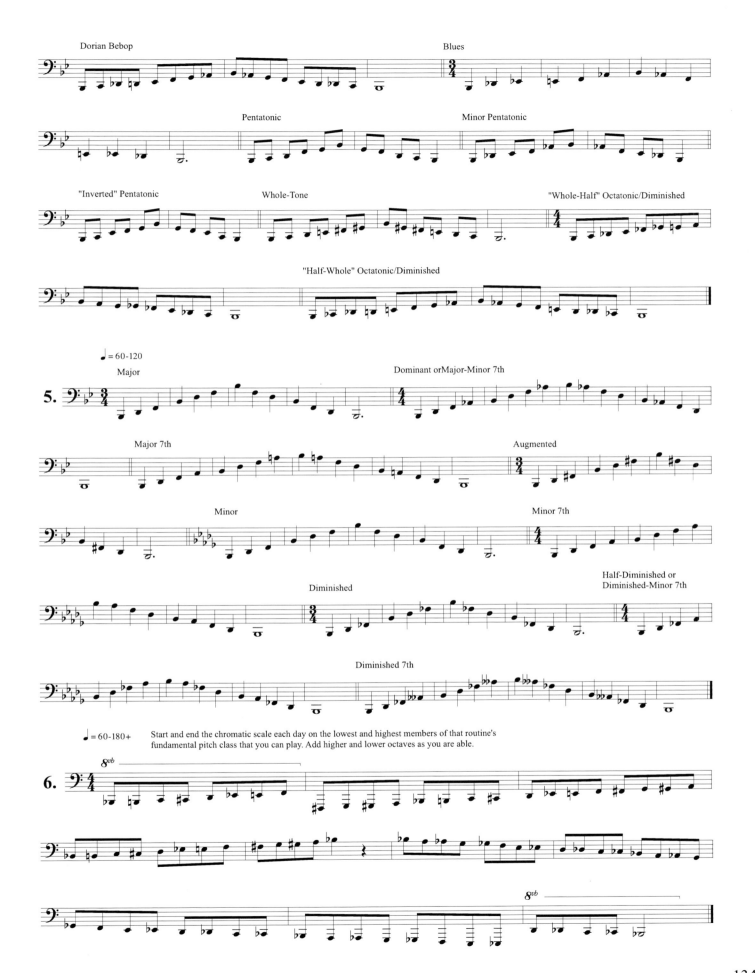

Appendix C: Bass Trombone Resources

Bass Trombone (B-flat/F/G-flat/D) Targeted Fundamentals

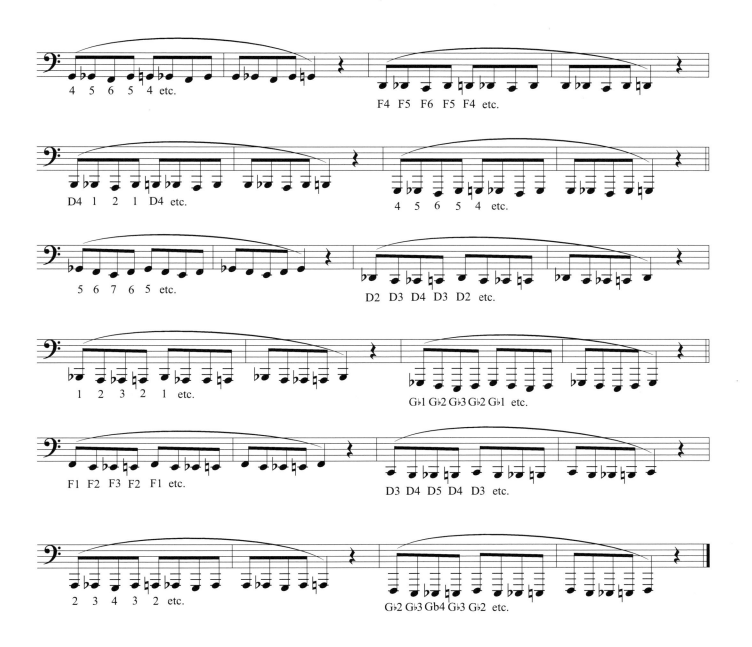

In the following exercise, stick with slower tempos when you are new to the instrument, increasing speed only when you become more comfortable with the slotting of the different partials.

Continue pattern through 7th position.

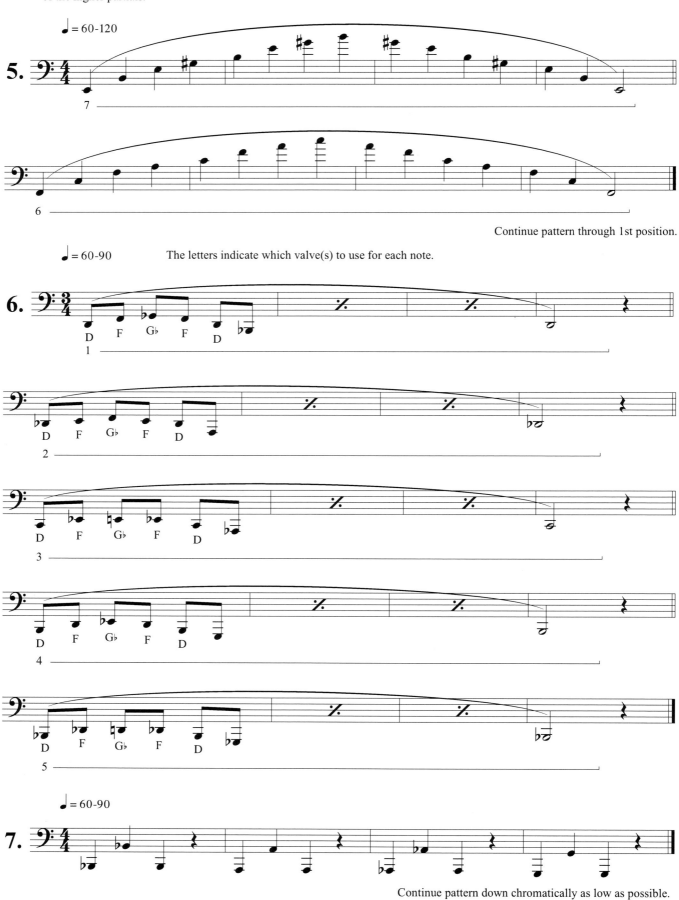

Bass Trombone (B-flat/F/G/E-flat) Targeted Fundamentals

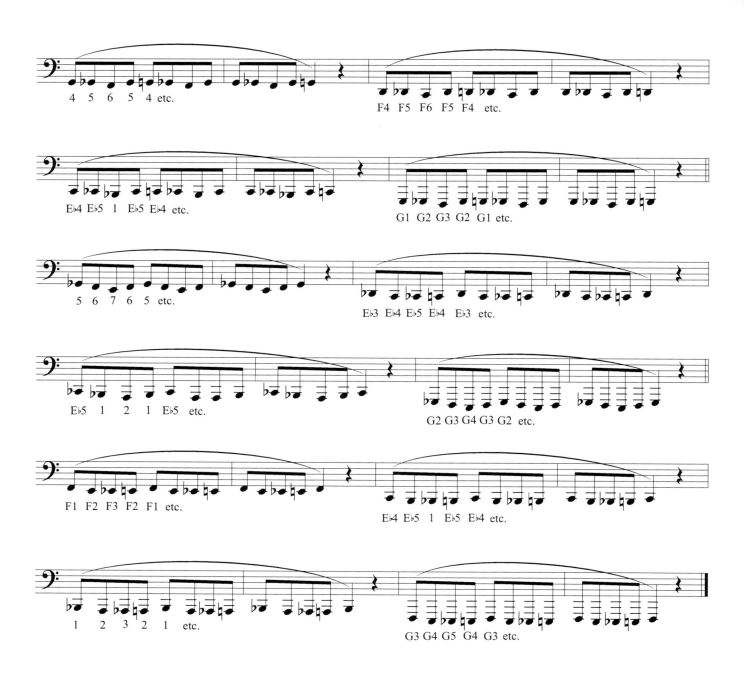

In the following exercise, stick with slower tempos when you are new to the instrument, increasing speed only when you become more comfortable with the slotting of the different partials.

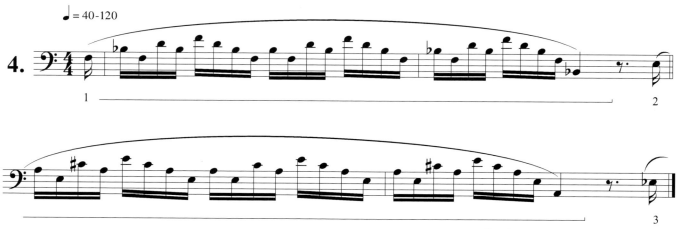

Continue pattern through 7th position.

In the next activity, if you are not able to reach the highest notes, play as high as you can, extending past your current comfort zone but not to the point of pain. Conversely, add notes to extend the range higher if necessary, and/or add lip trills to some of the higher partials.

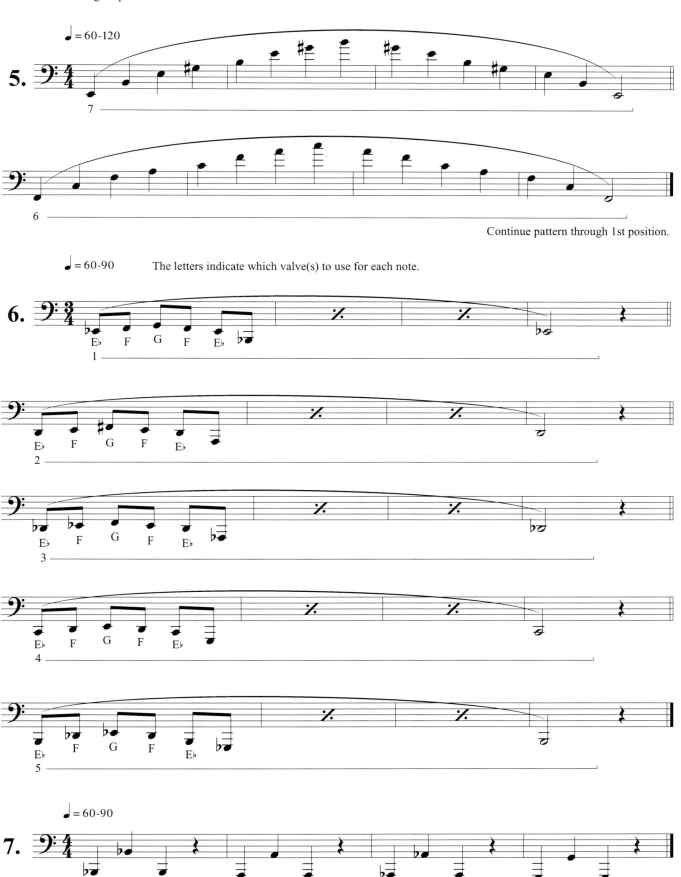

Bass Trombone (B-flat/F/G-flat/D) Slide Positions

In this chart, the commonly used positions are listed in order of preference. Tuning adjustments are noted only in the more extreme cases. For more comprehensive information about alternate positions and tuning adjustments, consult the overtone series chart.

Number Only = Open (no valves engaged)
F (number) = Position with F attachment engaged
G♭ (number) = Position with G♭ attachment engaged
D (number) = Position with both valves engaged

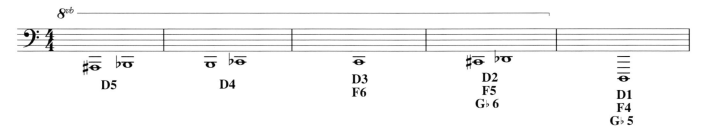

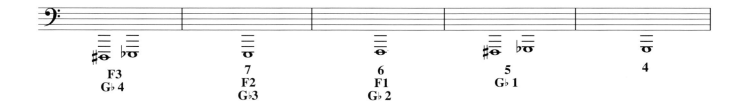

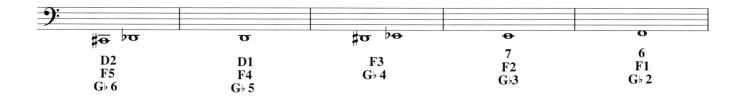

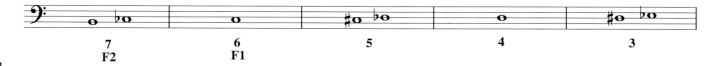

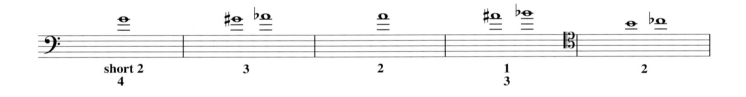

Bass Trombone (B-flat/F/G/E-flat) Slide Positions

In this chart, the commonly used positions are listed in order of preference. Tuning adjustments are noted only in the more extreme cases. For more comprehensive information about alternate positions and tuning adjustments, consult the overtone series chart.

Number Only = Open (no valves engaged)
F (number) = Position with F attachment engaged
G (number) = Position with G attachment engaged
E♭ (number) = Position with both valves engaged

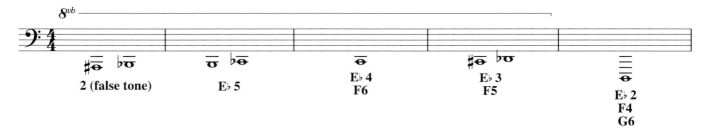

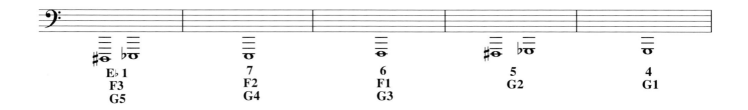

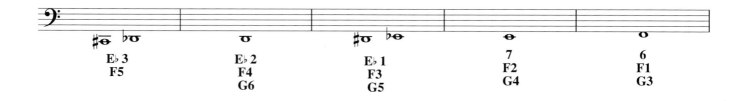

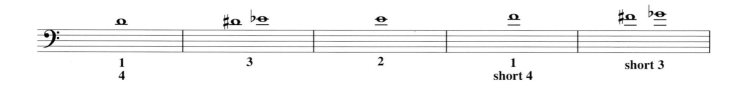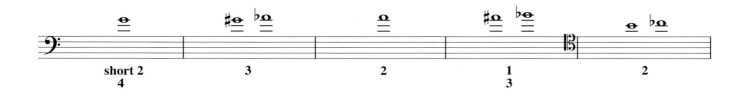

Bass Trombone (B-flat/F/G-flat/D) Overtone Series

Partial/Intonation Tendency →

Number Only = Open; No valves engaged
G♭ (number) = Position with G♭ attachment engaged
F (number) = Position with F attachment engaged
D (number) = Position with D attachment (combined F and G-flat attachments) engaged

Bass Trombone (B-flat/F/G/E-flat) Overtone Series

Number Only = Open; No valves engaged
G (number) = Position with G attachment engaged
F (number) = Position with F attachment engaged
E♭ (number) = Position with E♭ attachment (combined F and G attachments) engaged

146

Appendix D: Tenor Trombone Resources

Tenor Trombone Targeted Fundamentals

In the following exercise, stick with slower tempos when you are new to the instrument, increasing speed only when you become more comfortable with the slotting of the different partials.

Continue pattern through 7th position.

In the next activity, if you are not able to reach the highest notes, play as high as you can, extending past your current comfort zone but not to the point of pain. Conversely, add notes to extend the range higher if necessary, and/or add lip trills to some of the higher partials.

Continue pattern through 1st position.

Continue pattern down chromatically as low as possible.

Tenor Trombone Slide Positions

In this chart, the commonly used positions are listed in order of preference. Tuning adjustments are noted only in the more extreme cases. For more comprehensive information about alternate positions and tuning adjustments, consult the overtone series chart.

Number Only = Open (F valve not engaged)
F (number) = Position with F attachment engaged

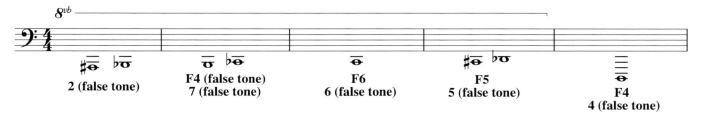

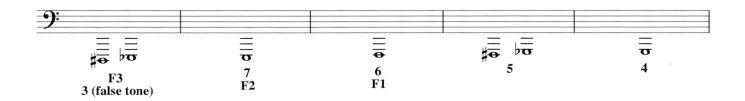

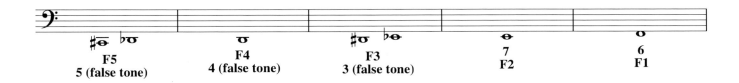

150

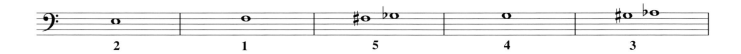

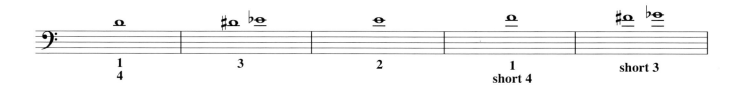
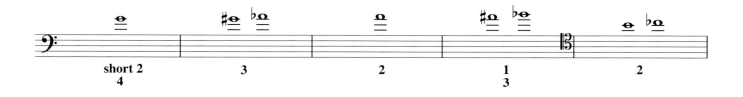
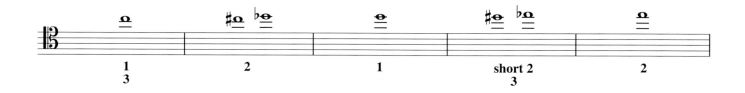

151

Tenor Trombone Overtone Series

Number Only = Open; No valves engaged
F (number) = Position with F attachment engaged

Appendix E: Euphonium and Baritone Horn Resources

Euphonium and Baritone Horn Targeted Fundamentals

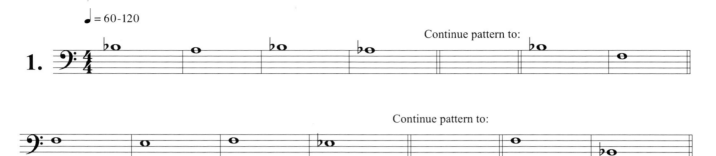

In the following exercise, stick with slower tempos when you are new to the instrument, increasing speed only when you become more comfortable with the slotting of the different partials.

Continue pattern through at least the 2-4 fingering.

153

In the next activity, if you are not able to reach the highest notes, play as high as you can, extending past your current comfort zone but not to the point of pain. Conversely, add notes to extend the range higher if necessary, and/or add lip trills to some of the higher partials.

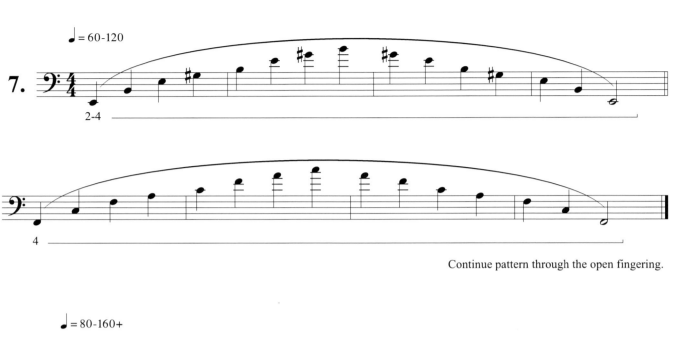

Continue pattern through the open fingering.

Continue pattern to:

Continue pattern down chromatically as low as possible.

Euphonium and Baritone Horn Fingerings

In this chart, the commonly used fingerings are listed in order of preference. For more comprehensive information about alternate fingerings, consult the overtone series chart.

C = Compensating
NC = Non-Compensating

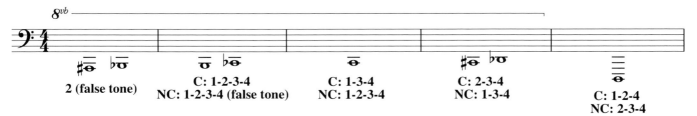
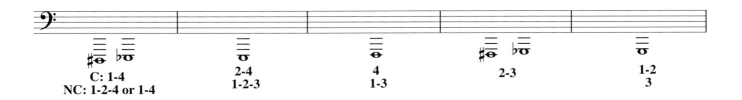

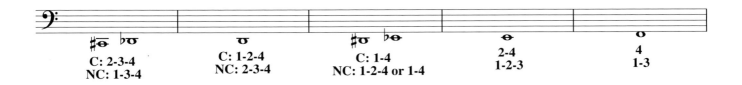

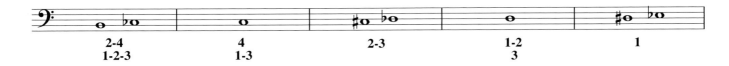

156

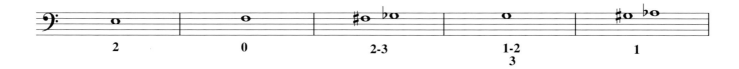

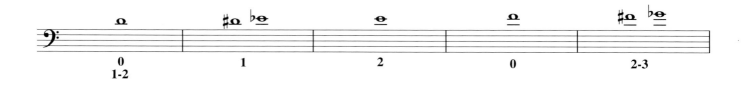
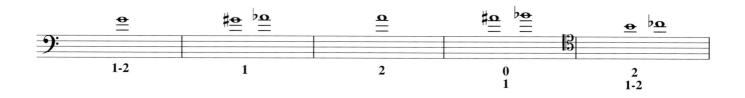
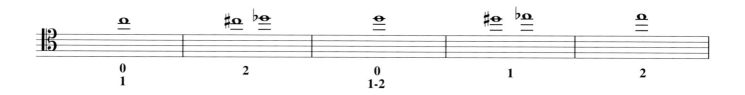

Euphonium and Baritone Horn Overtone Series

158

Appendix F: Tuba and Cimbasso Resources

BB-flat Tuba and Cimbasso Targeted Fundamentals

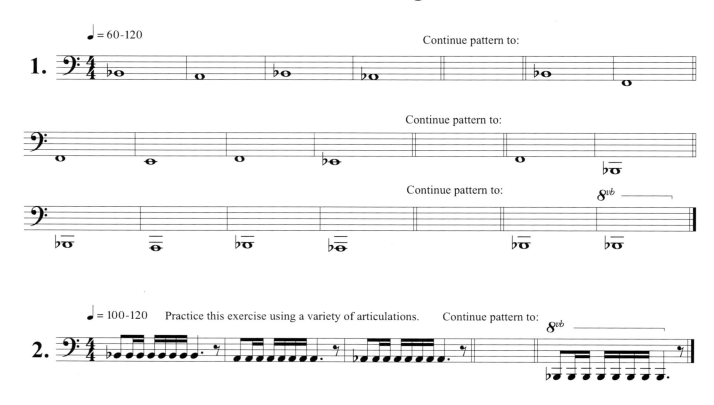

In the next activity, if you are not able to reach the highest notes, play as high as you can, extending past your current comfort zone but not to the point of pain. Conversely, add notes to extend the range higher if necessary, and/or add lip trills to some of the higher partials.

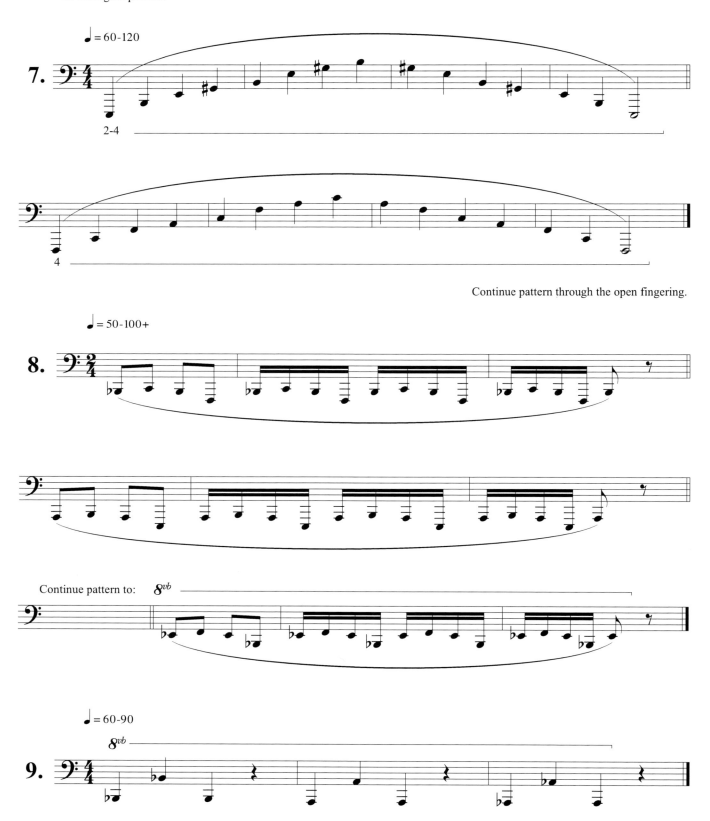

161

CC Tuba and Cimbasso Targeted Fundamentals

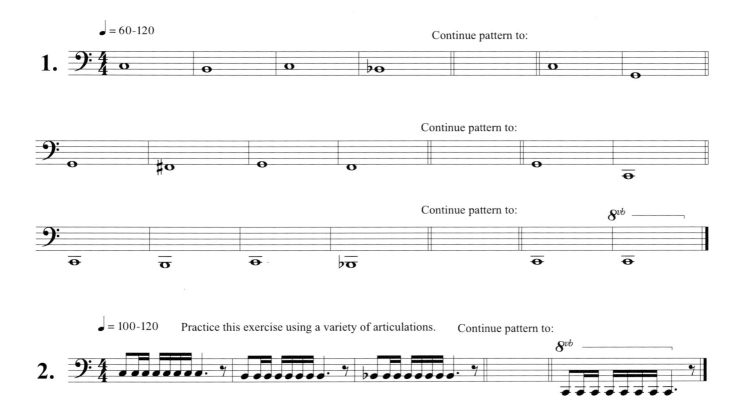

Continue pattern through at least the 2-4 fingering.

In the next activity, if you are not able to reach the highest notes, play as high as you can, extending past your current comfort zone but not to the point of pain. Conversely, add notes to extend the range higher if necessary, and/or add lip trills to some of the higher partials.

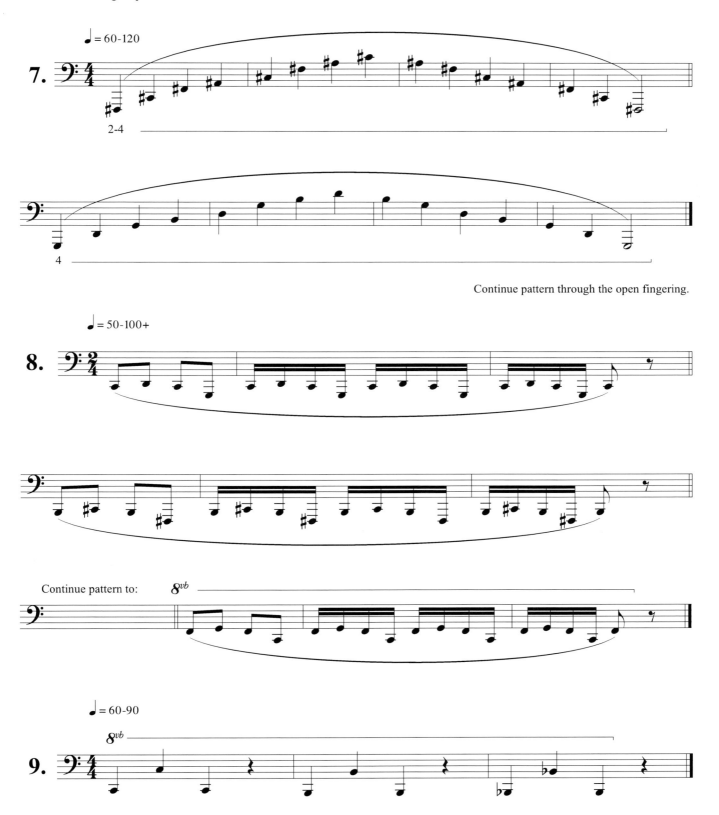

E-flat Tuba and Cimbasso Targeted Fundamentals

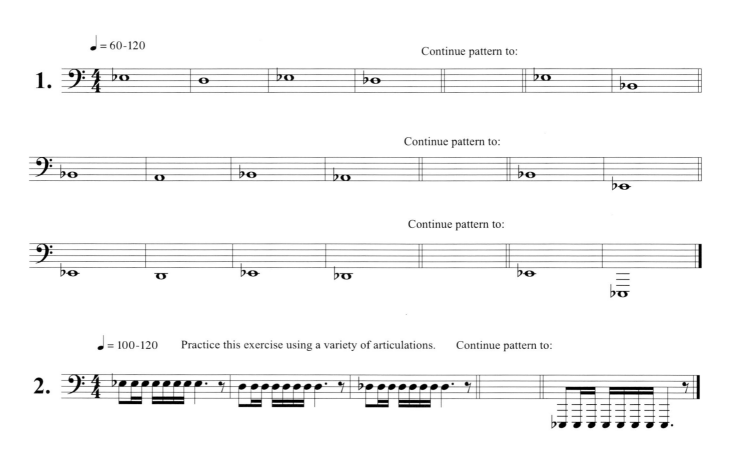

In the following exercise, stick with slower tempos when you are new to the instrument, increasing speed only when you become more comfortable with the slotting of the different partials.

In the next activity, if you are not able to reach the highest notes, play as high as you can, extending past your current comfort zone but not to the point of pain. Conversely, add notes to extend the range higher if necessary, and/or add lip trills to some of the higher partials.

7.

2-4

4

Continue pattern through the open fingering.

8.

Continue pattern to:

9.

Continue pattern down chromatically as low as possible.

F Tuba and Cimbasso Targeted Fundamentals

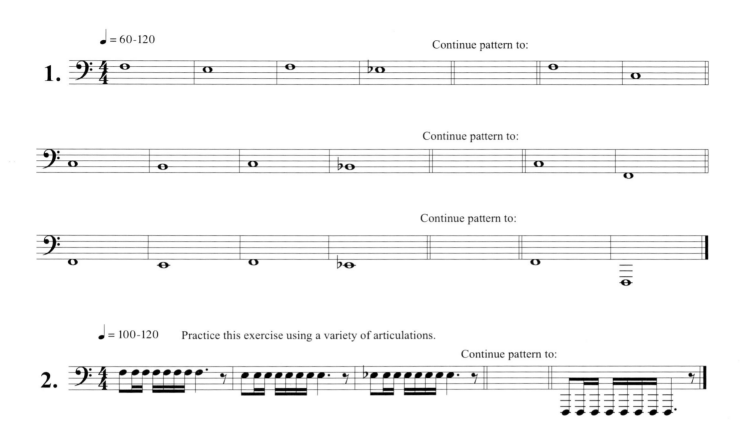

Continue pattern at least through the 2-4 fingering.

In the next activity, if you are not able to reach the highest notes, play as high as you can, extending past your current comfort zone but not to the point of pain. Conversely, add notes to extend the range higher if necessary, and/or add lip trills to some of the higher partials.

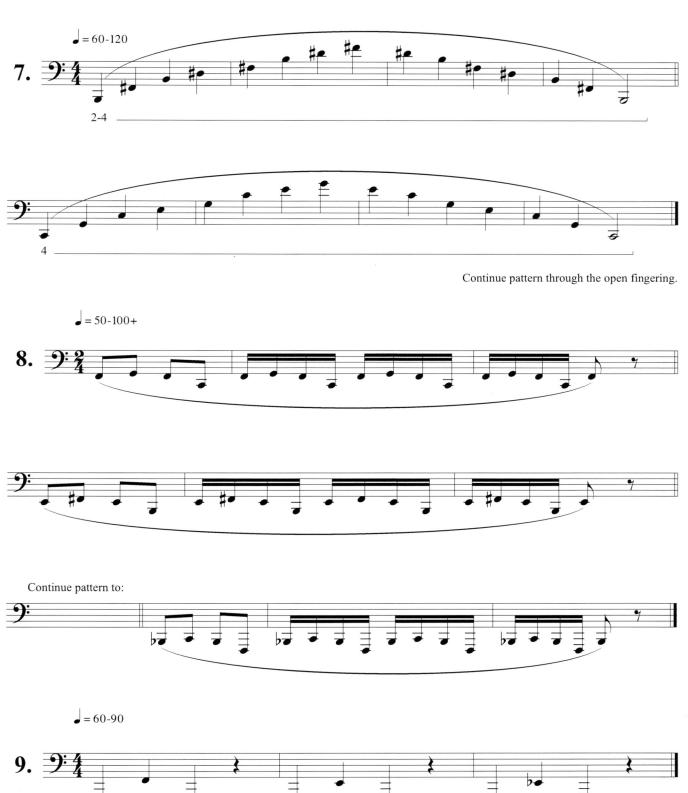

Continue pattern through the open fingering.

Continue pattern to:

Continue pattern down chromatically as low as possible.

BB-Flat Tuba and Cimbasso Fingerings

In this chart, the commonly used fingerings are listed in order of preference. For more comprehensive information about alternate fingerings, consult the overtone series chart.

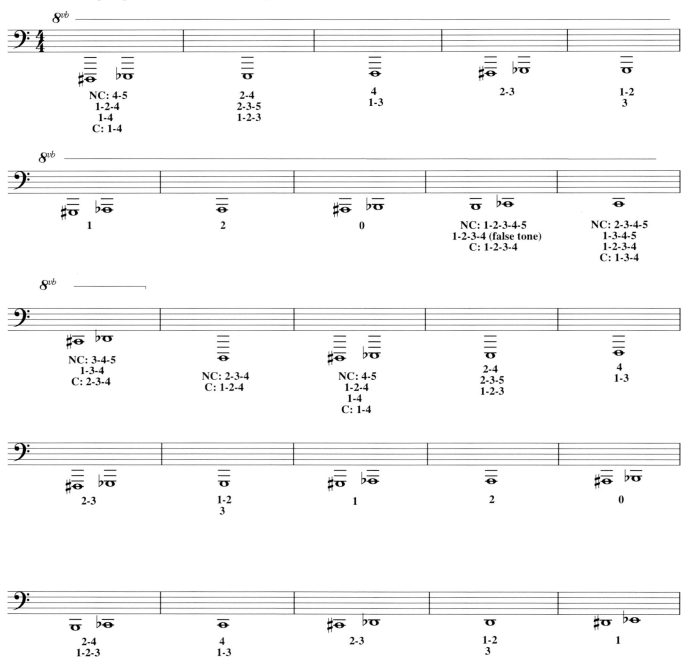

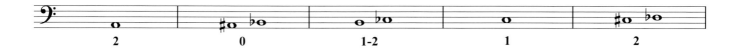

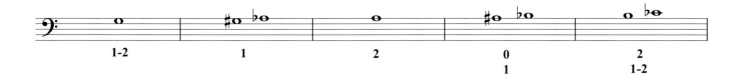
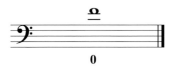

CC Tuba and Cimbasso Fingerings

In this chart, the commonly used fingerings are listed in order of preference. For more comprehensive information about alternate fingerings, consult the overtone series chart.

Fifth valve fingerings are for a flat whole step fifth valve

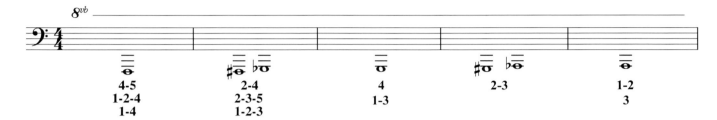

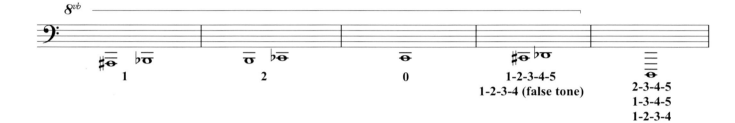

173

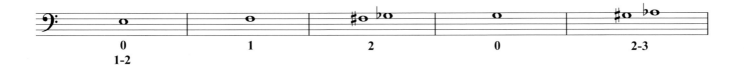
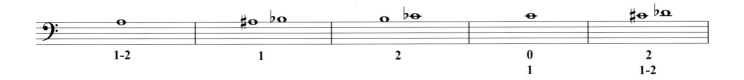
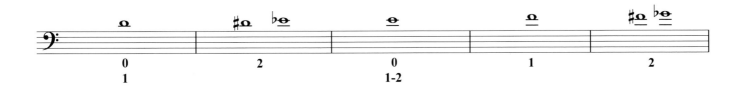
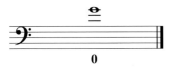

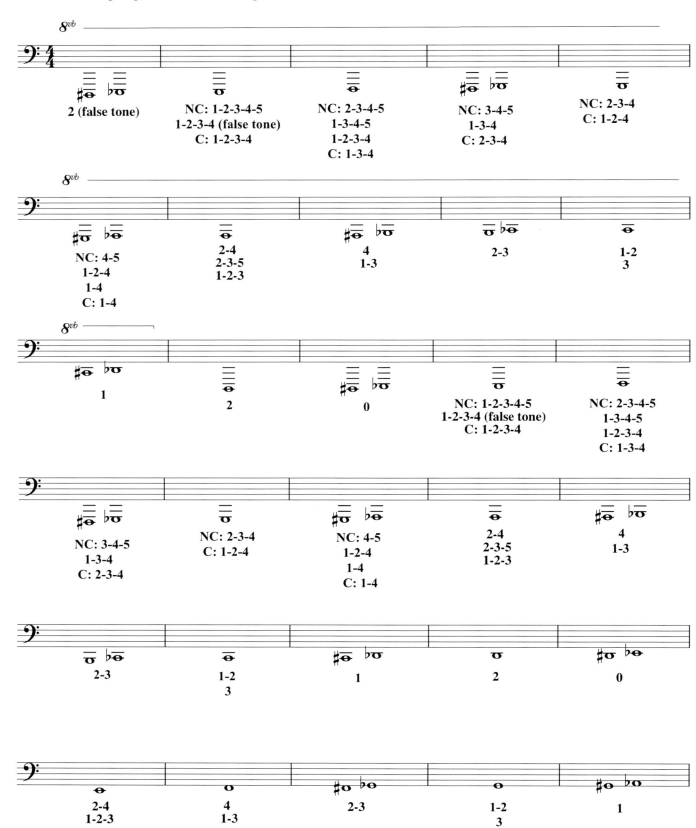

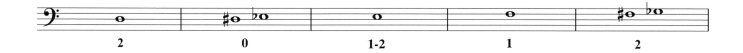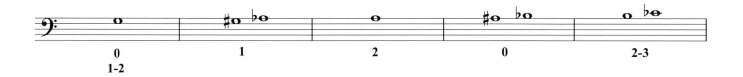

F Tuba and Cimbasso Fingerings

In this chart, the commonly used fingerings are listed in order of preference. For more comprehensive information about alternate fingerings, consult the overtone series chart.

Fifth valve fingerings are for a flat whole step fifth valve

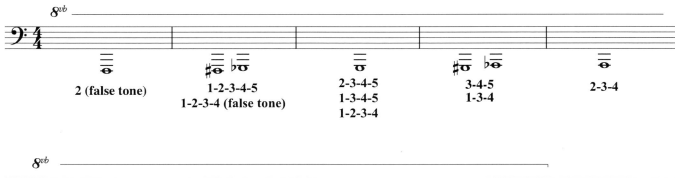

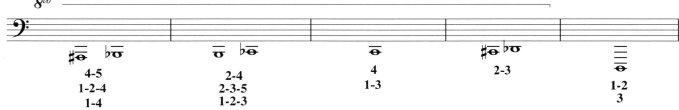

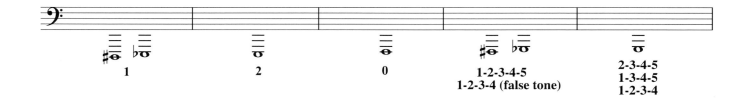

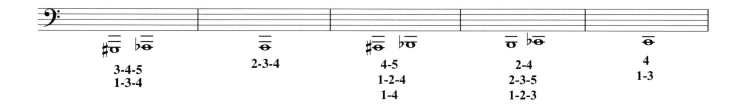

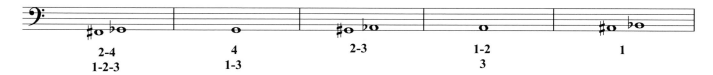

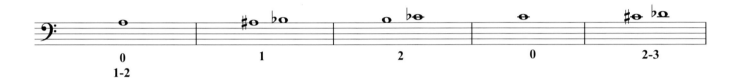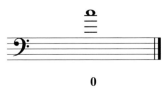

BB-flat Tuba and Cimbasso Overtone Series

Partial/
Intonation Tendency

Fingering →	0	2	1	1-2 or 3	2-3	4 or 1-3	2-4 1-2-3 2-3-5	NC: 4-5 1-2-4 1-4 C: 1-4	NC: 2-3-4 C: 1-2-4	NC: 3-4-5 1-3-4 C: 2-3-4	NC: 2-3-4-5 1-3-4-5 1-2-3-4 C: 1-3-4	NC: 1-2-3-4-5 Not present on four-valve instruments C: 1-2-3-4

12th Partial
(Sharp--Lower Slightly)

11th Partial
(Very Flat--Unusable)

10th Partial
(Flat--Raise Slightly)

9th Partial
(Sharp--Lower Slightly)

8th Partial
(Normal)

7th Partial
(Very Flat--Unusable)

6th Partial
(Sharp--Lower Slightly)

5th Partial
(Flat--Raise Slightly)

4th Partial
(Normal)

3rd Partial
(Sharp--Lower Slightly)

2nd Partial
(Normal)

Fundamental
(Normal)

Note: The fifth valve fingerings shown here are for a flat whole step fifth valve.

NC = Non-Compensating
C = Compensating

179

CC Tuba and Cimbasso Overtone Series

Note: The fifth valve fingerings shown here are for a flat whole step fifth valve.

180

E-flat Tuba and Cimbasso Overtone Series

Note: The fifth valve fingerings shown here are for a flat whole step fifth valve.

NC = Non-Compensating
C = Compensating

F Tuba and Cimbasso Overtone Series

Partial/Intonation Tendency	0	2	1	1-2 or 3	2-3	4 or 1-3	2-4 / 1-2-3 / 2-3-5	4-5 / 1-2-4 / 1-4	2-3-4	3-4-5 / 1-3-4	2-3-4-5 / 1-3-4-5 / 1-2-3-4	1-2-3-4-5 Not present on four-valve instruments.
12th Partial (Sharp--Lower Slightly)												
11th Partial (Very Flat--Unusable)												
10th Partial (Flat--Raise Slightly)												
9th Partial (Sharp--Lower Slightly)												
8th Partial (Normal)												
7th Partial (Very Flat--Unusable)												
6th Partial (Sharp--Lower Slightly)												
5th Partial (Flat--Raise Slightly)												
4th Partial (Normal)												
3rd Partial (Sharp--Lower Slightly)												
2nd Partial (Normal)												
Fundamental (Normal)												

Note: The fifth valve fingerings shown here are for a flat whole step fifth valve.

Appendix G: Alto Trombone Resources

Alto Trombone Targeted Fundamentals

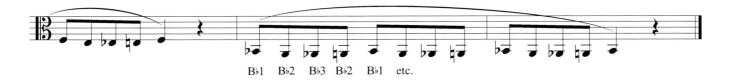

In the following exercise, stick with slower tempos when you are new to the instrument, increasing speed only when you become more comfortable with the slotting of the different partials.

Continue pattern through 7th position.

184

In the next activity, if you are not able to reach the highest notes, play as high as you can, extending past your current comfort zone but not to the point of pain. Conversely, add notes to extend the range higher if necessary, and/or add lip trills to some of the higher partials.

Continue pattern through 1st position.

Continue pattern down chromatically as low as possible.

Alto Trombone Slide Positions

In this chart, the commonly used positions are listed in order of preference. Tuning adjustments are noted only in the more extreme cases. For more comprehensive information about alternate positions and tuning adjustments, consult the overtone series chart.

Number Only = Open (B♭ valve not engaged)
B♭ (number) = Position with B♭ attachment engaged

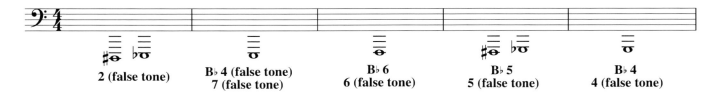

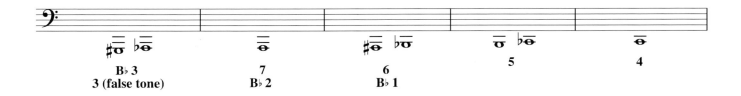

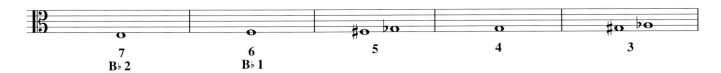

186

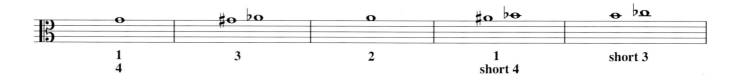

Alto Trombone Overtone Series

188

Appendix H: Contrabass Trombone Resources

Contrabass Trombone (F/C/D-flat/AA) Targeted Fundamentals

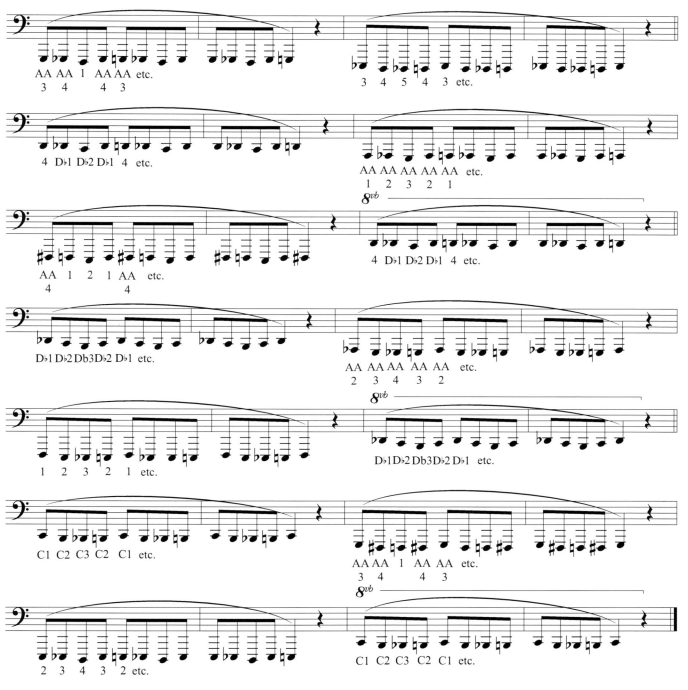

In the following exercise, stick with slower tempos when you are new to the instrument, increasing speed only when you become more comfortable with the slotting of the different partials.

Continue pattern through 5th position, or through positions with valves, if desired.

In the next activity, if you are not able to reach the highest notes, play as high as you can, extending past your current comfort zone but not to the point of pain. Conversely, add notes to extend the range higher if necessary, and/or add lip trills to some of the higher partials.

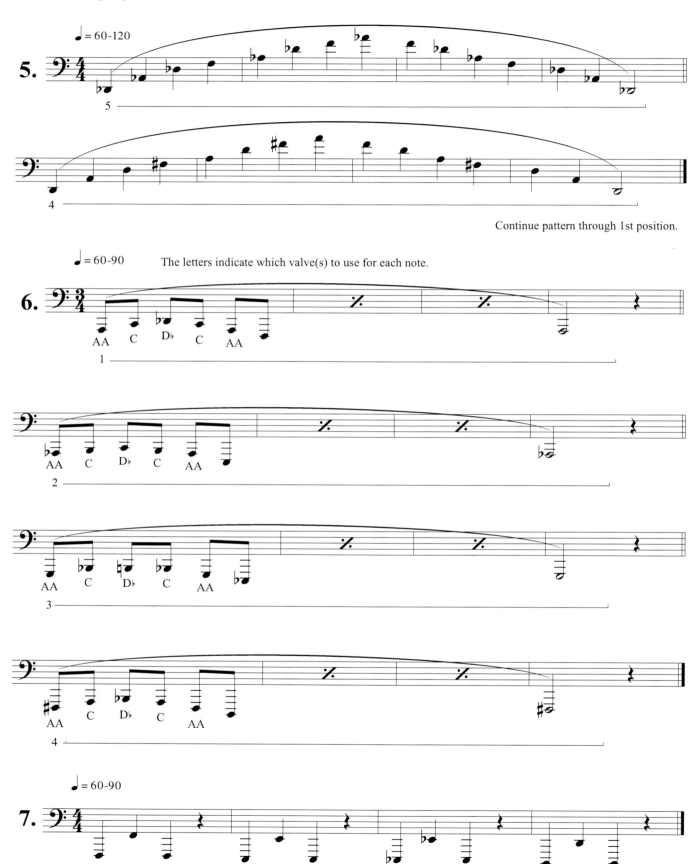

Continue pattern through 1st position.

The letters indicate which valve(s) to use for each note.

Continue pattern down chromatically as low as possible.

Contrabass Trombone (F/D/B-flat/AA-flat) Targeted Fundamentals

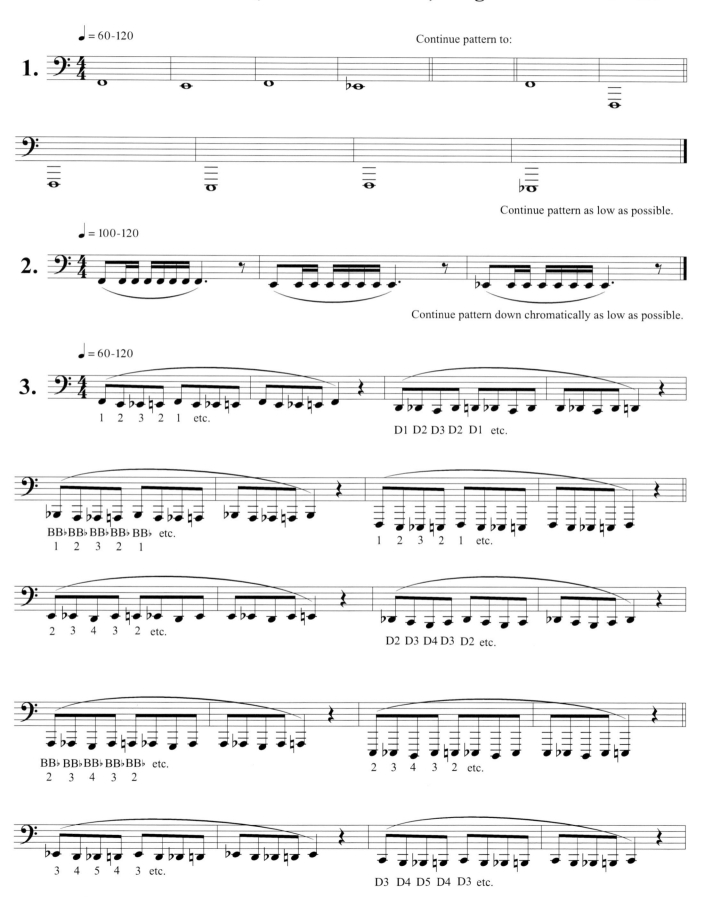

192

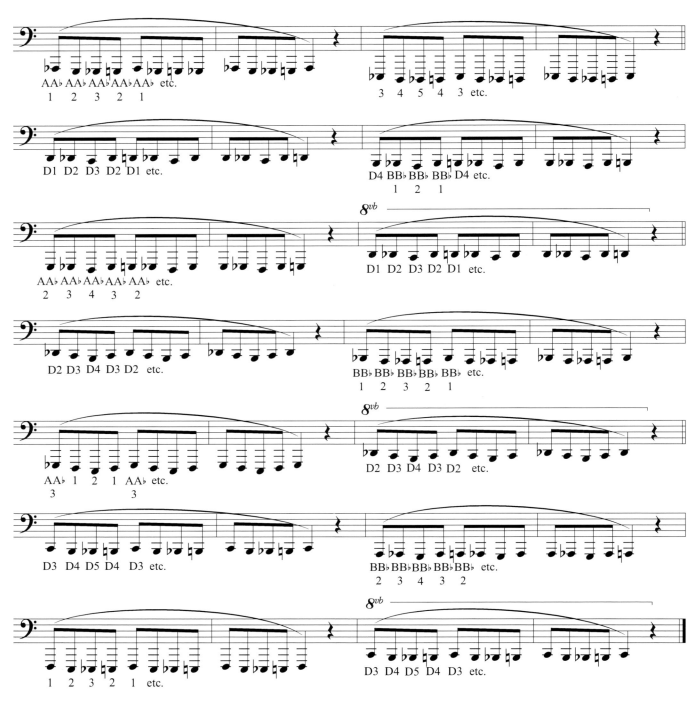

In the following exercise, stick with slower tempos when you are new to the instrument, increasing speed only when you become more comfortable with the slotting of the different partials.

Continue pattern through 5th position, or through positions with valves, if desired.

In the next activity, if you are not able to reach the highest notes, play as high as you can, extending past your current comfort zone but not to the point of pain. Conversely, add notes to extend the range higher if necessary, and/or add lip trills to some of the higher partials.

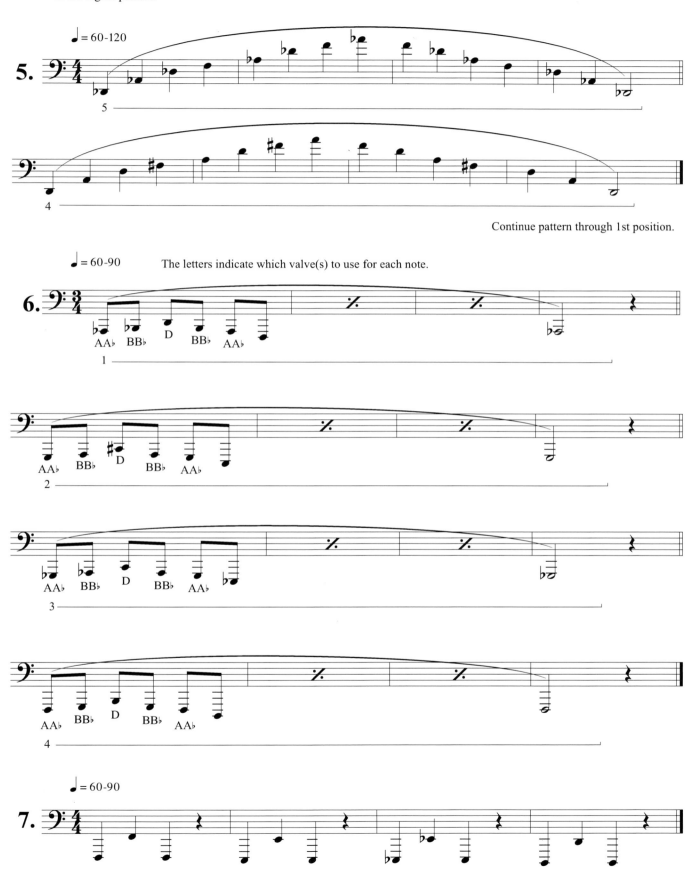

Continue pattern through 1st position.

Continue pattern down chromatically as low as possible.

194

Contrabass Trombone (F/C/D-flat/AA) Fingerings

In this chart, the commonly used positions are listed in order of preference. Tuning adjustments are noted only in the more extreme cases. For more comprehensive information about alternate positions and tuning adjustments, consult the overtone series chart.

Number Only = Open (no valves engaged)
D♭ (number) = Position with D♭ attachment engaged
C (number) = Position with C attachment engaged
AA (number) = Position with both valves engaged

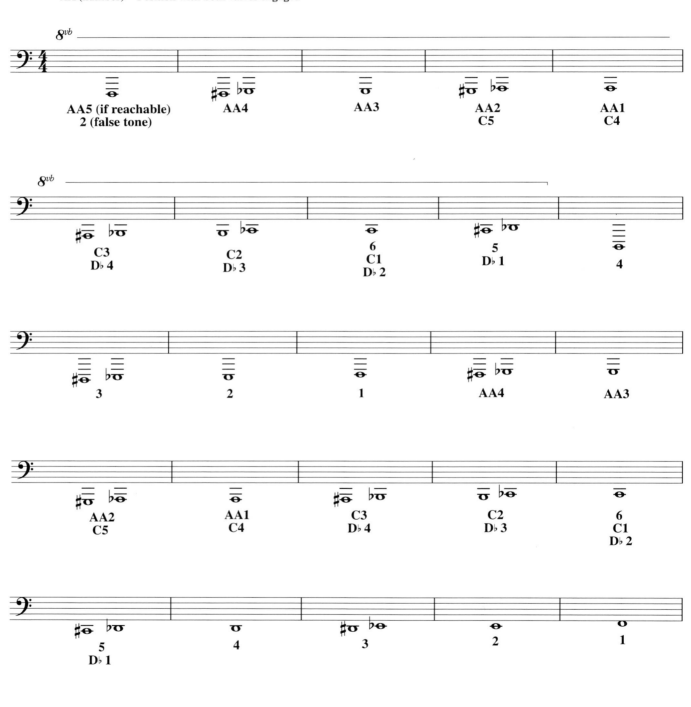

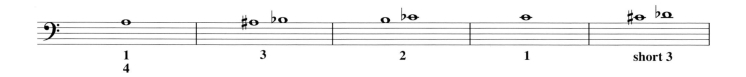
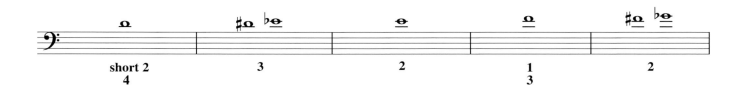
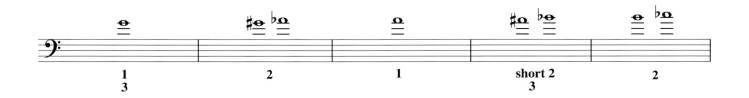

Contrabass Trombone (F/D/BB-flat/AA-flat) Fingerings

In this chart, the commonly used positions are listed in order of preference. Tuning adjustments are noted only in the more extreme cases. For more comprehensive information about alternate positions and tuning adjustments, consult the overtone series chart.

Number Only = Open (no valves engaged)
D (number) = Position with D attachment engaged
BB♭ (number) = Position with BB♭ attachment engaged
AA♭ (number) = Position with both valves engaged

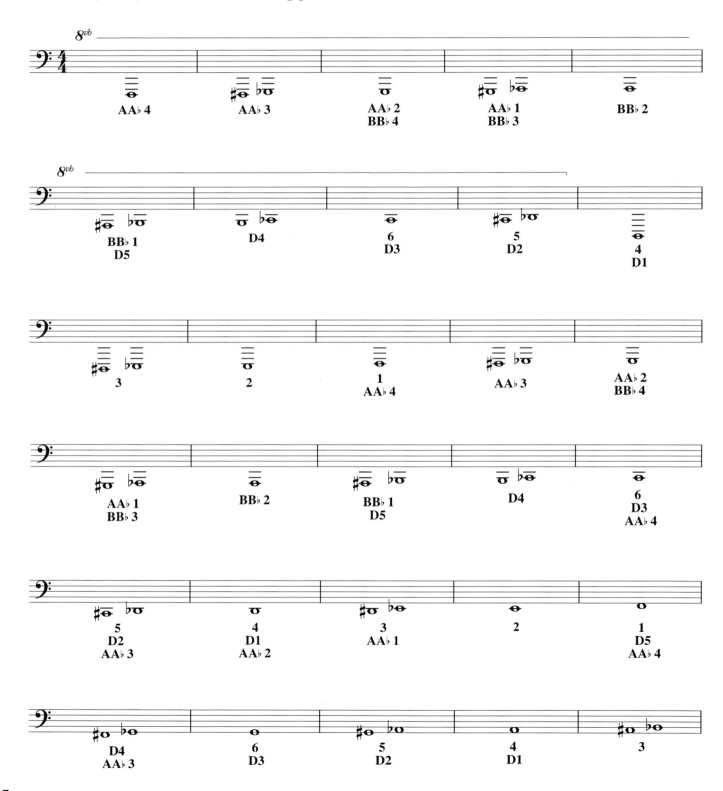

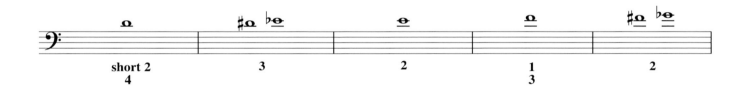

Contrabass Trombone (F/C/D-flat/AA) Overtone Series

Partial/Intonation Tendency →

Partial / Intonation Tendency	1	2	3	4	5 or D♭ 1	6 D♭ 2 C1	7* D♭ 3 C2	D♭ 4 C3	D♭ 5 C4 AA1	D♭ 6* C5 AA2	C6* AA3	AA4
12th Partial (Sharp--Lower Slightly)												
11th Partial (Very Flat--Raise Much; First Position Unusable)												
10th Partial (Flat--Raise Slightly)												
9th Partial (Sharp--Lower Slightly)												
8th Partial (Normal)												
7th Partial (Very Flat--Raise Much; First Position Unusable)												
6th Partial (Sharp--Lower Slightly)												
5th Partial (Flat--Raise Slightly)												
4th Partial (Normal)												
3rd Partial (Sharp--Lower Slightly)												
2nd Partial (Normal)												
Fundamental (Normal)												

Slide Position/Fingering → 1

Number Only = Open; No valves engaged
D♭ (number) = Position with D♭ attachment engaged
C (number) = Position with C attachment engaged
AA (number) = Position with AA attachment (combined C and D♭ attachments) engaged

* These positions may be out of reach without a handle attached to the handslide and might be absent entirely on some models. They are listed for the sake of thoroughness but these outer positions are more theoretical than practical.

Contrabass Trombone (F/D/BB-flat/AA-flat) Overtone Series

Partial/Intonation Tendency

12th Partial (Sharp—Lower Slightly)

11th Partial (Very Flat—Raise Much; First Position Unusable)

10th Partial (Flat—Raise Slightly)

9th Partial (Sharp—Lower Slightly)

8th Partial (Normal)

7th Partial (Very Flat—Raise Much; First Position Unusable)

6th Partial (Sharp—Lower Slightly)

5th Partial (Flat—Raise Slightly)

4th Partial (Normal)

3rd Partial (Sharp—Lower Slightly)

2nd Partial (Normal)

Fundamental (Normal)

Slide Position/Fingering →

| 1 | 2 | 3 | 4 or D1 | 5 or D2 | 6 or D3 | 7* or D4 | D5 BB♭ 1 | D6* BB♭ 2 | BB♭ 3 AA♭ 1 | BB♭ 4 AA♭ 2 | BB♭ 5* AA♭ 3 | AA♭ 4 |

Number Only = Open; No valves engaged
D (number) = Position with D attachment engaged
BB♭ (number) = Position with BB♭ attachment engaged
AA♭ (number) = Position with AA♭ attachment (combined D and BB♭ attachments) engaged

* These positions may be out of reach without a handle attached to the handslide and might be absent entirely on some models. They are listed for the sake of thoroughness but these outer positions are more theoretical than practical.

200

Appendix I: Bass Trumpet Resources

B-flat Bass Trumpet Targeted Fundamentals

Sounding pitches one octave lower than written

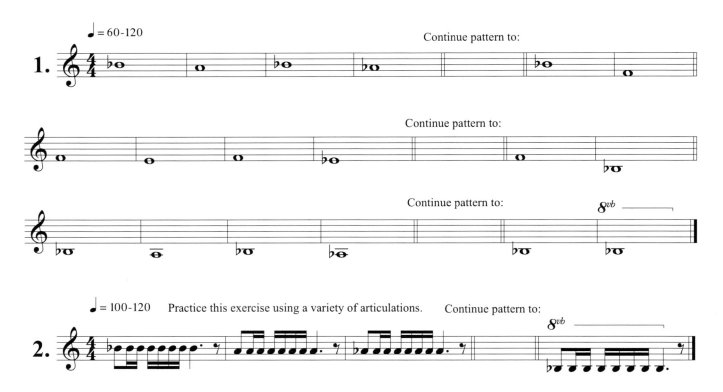

In the following exercise, stick with slower tempos when you are new to the instrument, increasing speed only when you become more comfortable with the slotting of the different partials.

In the next activity, if you are not able to reach the highest notes, play as high as you can, extending past your current comfort zone but not to the point of pain. Conversely, add notes to extend the range higher if necessary, and/or add lip trills to some of the higher partials.

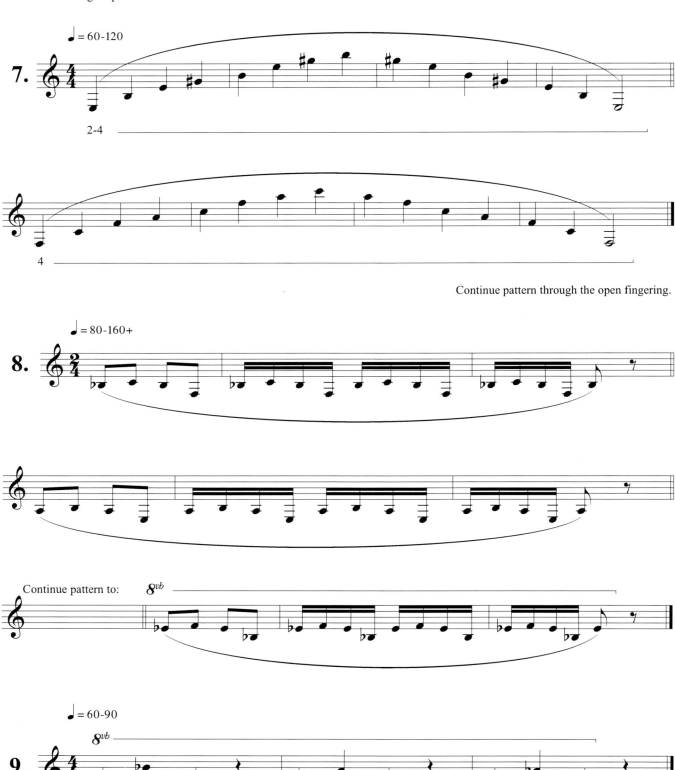

C Bass Trumpet Targeted Fundamentals

Sounding pitches are one octave lower than written.

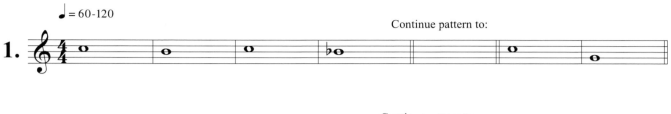

In the following exercise, stick with slower tempos when you are new to the instrument, increasing speed only when you become more comfortable with the slotting of the different partials.

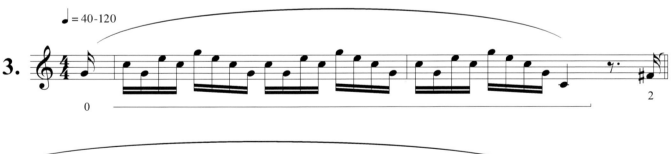

Continue pattern at least through the 2-4 fingering.

In the next activity, if you are not able to reach the highest notes, play as high as you can, extending past your current comfort zone but not to the point of pain. Conversely, add notes to extend the range higher if necessary, and/or add lip trills to some of the higher partials.

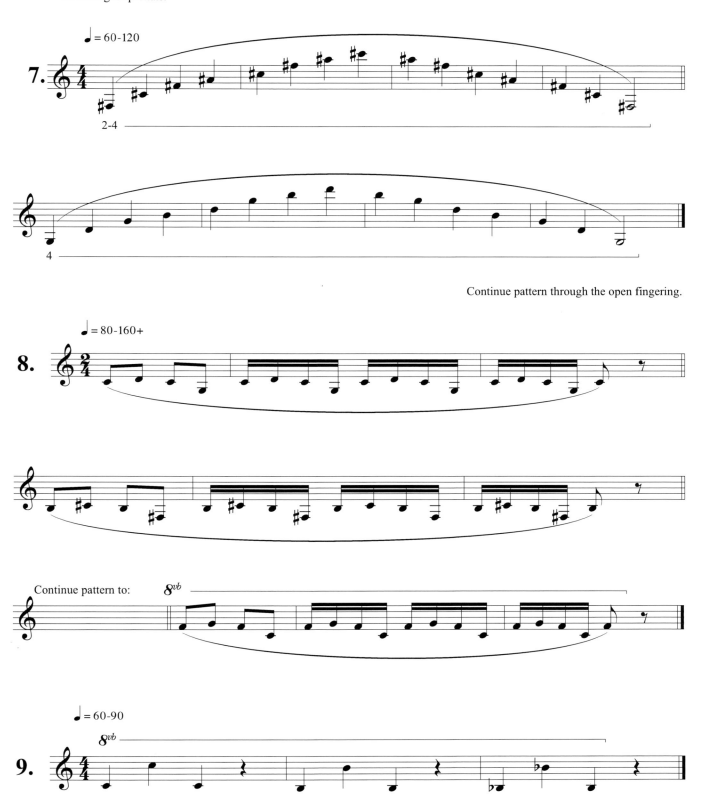

B-flat Bass Trumpet Fingerings

This is a *concert pitch* chart, with the sounding pitches one octave lower than written.

In this chart, the commonly used fingerings are listed in order of preference. For more comprehensive information about alternate fingerings, consult the overtone series chart.

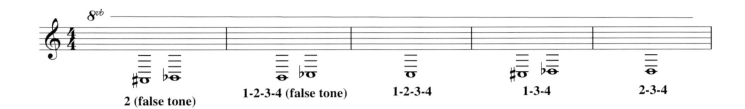

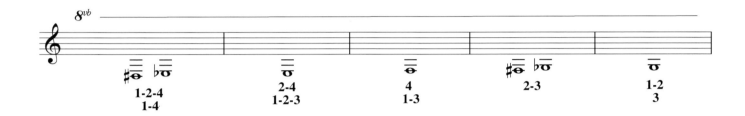

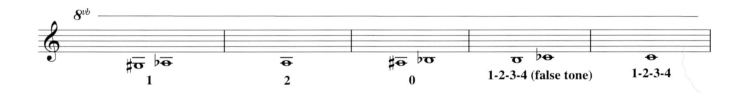

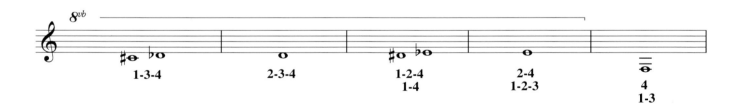

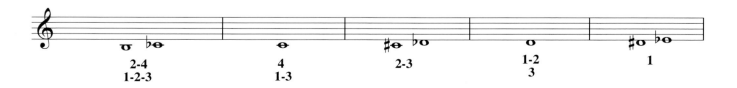

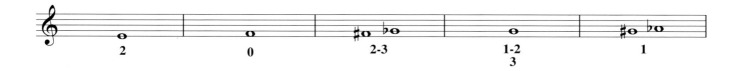

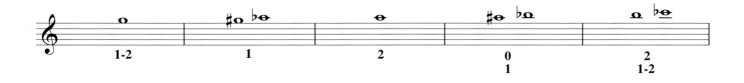

C Bass Trumpet Fingerings

This is a *concert pitch* chart, with the sounding pitches one octave lower than written.

In this chart, the commonly used fingerings are listed in order of preference. For more comprehensive information about alternate fingerings, consult the overtone series chart.

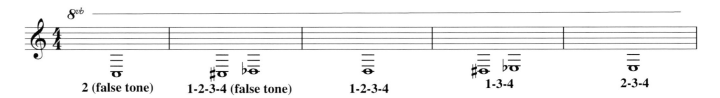

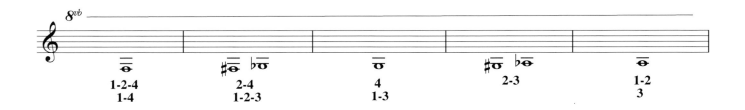

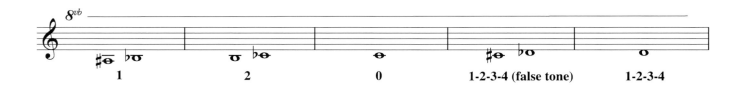

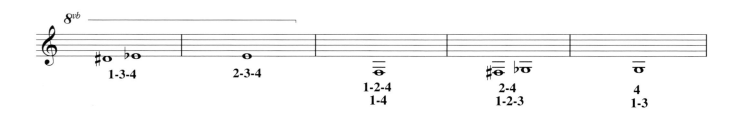

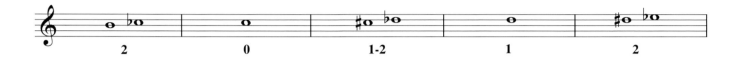

B-flat Bass Trumpet Overtone Series

Note: This is a *concert pitch* chart, with the sounding pitches one octave lower than written.

C Bass Trumpet Overtone Series

Note: This is a *concert pitch* chart, with the sounding pitches one octave lower than written.

Partial/ Intonation Tendency →

Partial / Intonation Tendency
12th Partial (Sharp--Lower Slightly)
11th Partial (Very Flat--Unusable)
10th Partial (Flat--Raise Slightly)
9th Partial (Sharp--Lower Slightly)
8th Partial (Normal)
7th Partial (Very Flat--Unusable)
6th Partial (Sharp--Lower Slightly)
5th Partial (Flat--Raise Slightly)
4th Partial (Normal)
3rd Partial (Sharp--Lower Slightly)
2nd Partial (Normal)
Fundamental (Normal)

Fingering → 0   2   1   1-2 or 3   2-3   4 or 1-3   2-4 or 1-2-3   1-2-4 or 1-4   2-3-4   1-3-4   1-2-3-4

About the Authors

Dr. Micah Everett is Assistant Professor of Music at the University of Mississippi, where he teaches applied trombone, euphonium, and tuba, conducts the trombone ensemble and tuba-euphonium ensemble, and teaches the undergraduate low brass methods course as well as graduate courses in brass literature and brass pedagogy. A Mississippi native, he received the Bachelor of Music Education degree from Delta State University, where he studied trombone and euphonium with Edward R. Bahr. He holds Master of Music and Doctor of Musical Arts degrees from the University of North Carolina at Greensboro (UNCG), where he studied trombone with Randy Kohlenberg, and euphonium and tuba with Dennis AsKew. Prior to joining the Ole Miss faculty in 2012, Dr. Everett was Associate Professor of Music at the University of Louisiana at Monroe, and also held teaching positions at the University of Northern Iowa, Elon University, and UNCG.

An active recitalist, orchestral, and chamber musician on alto, tenor, and bass trombones and euphonium, Dr. Everett is currently principal trombonist in the North Mississippi Symphony Orchestra, trombonist in the Mississippi Brass Quintet, and bass trombonist in the Great River Trombone Quartet. He is a past winner of the National Solo Competition held at the Eastern Trombone Workshop, and has performed more than twenty times as a featured soloist with bands and orchestras in Mississippi, Louisiana, Arkansas, Alabama, North Carolina, and Iowa. He has appeared as clinician, soloist, or conductor at the International Trombone Festival, the Eastern Trombone Workshop, the South Central and Mid-South Regional Tuba Euphonium Conferences, and numerous other regional conferences and workshops.

Dr. Everett is an active member of the International Trombone Association (ITA), currently serving as Assistant Editor (audio/video reviews) for the *International Trombone Association Journal*. He serves as Mississippi Chairperson for the National Association of College Wind and Percussion Instructors, and is a member of the International Tuba Euphonium Association, the Historic Brass Society, the College Music Society, and the Pi Kappa Lambda, Phi Kappa Phi, and

Phi Eta Sigma National Honor Societies. His arrangements for brass soloists and ensembles have been published by Potenza Music, Cimarron Music, and TAP Music, and his articles and reviews have appeared in the *International Trombone Association Journal*, the *National Association of College Wind and Percussion Instructors Journal*, *The Instrumentalist*, and Conn-Selmer's *Keynotes Magazine*. He currently blogs at The Reforming Trombonist.

Jeff Cortazzo was appointed bass trombonist/tubist of The U.S. Army Blues in 1992. He is also currently bass trombonist in the National Philharmonic and bass/contrabass trombonist in the Capitol Bones, the Washington Trombone Ensemble, the Alan Baylock Jazz Orchestra, and often performs with the Smithsonian Jazz Masterworks and National Gallery Orchestras.

Mr. Cortazzo holds a Bachelor's degree in music education from West Chester University of Pennsylvania where he graduated magna cum laude, and a Master of Music degree in bass trombone performance from DePaul University in Chicago, also graduating magna cum laude. He is currently pursuing a Doctor of Musical Arts degree in Music Theory and Composition from The Catholic University of American in Washington, DC. As a published composer and member of ASCAP, many of his compositions, written for chamber groups to full orchestra and chorus, are available through BRS music publishers and have been performed in major concert halls in the United States, Europe, and China.

Mr. Cortazzo has performed with the Civic Orchestra of Chicago, the Chicago Symphony Orchestra, the National Sympnony Orchestra, the Baltimore Symphony Orchestra, and the Kennedy Center Opera Orchestra. He has also performed as bass trombonist/tubist with Frank Sinatra, Jr., Tony Bennett, Aretha Franklin, Barry Manilow, Yo Yo Ma, Joshua Bell, Itzhak Perlman and countless others. His principal teachers include Charles Vernon and Lee Southall for trombone, and Larry Nelson, Steven Gorbos, and Andrew Earle Simpson for composition and counterpoint.

Dr. Marc Dickman, from Valdosta, Georgia, is a founding member of the acclaimed jazz studies program at the University of North Florida (UNF). Dr. Dickman earned degrees from Troy State University, McNeese State University, and the University of North Texas. His versatility on

euphonium, trombone, bass trombone, and tuba in classical and jazz styles places him in much demand in the United States. At UNF he teaches applied low brass and jazz ensemble. He is a winner of the artist division of the Leonard Falcone International Euphonium and Tuba Festival Competition. Dr. Dickman was a featured jazz artist at the 2000 International Tuba Euphonium Conference (ITEC) in Regina, Saskatchewan, Canada, the 2001 ITEC in Lahti, Finland, the 2002 ITEC in Greensboro, North Carolina, and the 2004 ITEC in Budapest, Hungary. He was also a featured jazz artist at the 2005 and 2008 United States Army Tuba Euphonium Conferences.

Dr. Dickman is a founding member of the groundbreaking jazz ensemble, the Modern Jazz Tuba Project which has two critically acclaimed releases: Live From the Bottom Line and Favorite Things. Dr. Dickman's CD, A Weaver of Dreams is the first jazz euphonium recording available through popular services such as iTunes and RealNetworks.

Dr. Dickman hosted the 2013 Southeastern Regional Tuba Euphonium Conference at the University of North Florida. He plays trombone and leads the TBA Big Band, Jacksonville's only regularly performing professional jazz ensemble. He also subs for the Jacksonville Symphony Orchestra and the Gainesville Chamber Orchestra on bass trombone. Dr. Dickman has performed in Japan, Hungary, Finland, Paraguay, Uruguay, Canada, Honduras, and Columbia. Dr. Dickman is a Besson performing artist.

Brian French joined the Winston-Salem Symphony as principal trombonist in 2000, and made his Classics Series solo debut in February 2002. Brian has held principal positions in the Arkansas Symphony Orchestra and the Civic Orchestra of Chicago, and has performed frequently with the North Carolina Symphony. As a doubling musician, he has performed on tenor tuba and bass trumpet with the Winston-Salem Symphony, the

Greensboro Symphony Orchestra, the Roanoke Symphony and Opera, and the North Carolina Opera. Mr. French is on the music performance faculty of Wake Forest University.

Dr. Frank Gazda is Associate Professor of Music at Delaware State University in Dover, where he teaches applied low brass, music history, brass methods, and directs the trombone and tuba-euphonium ensembles. He is a former member of the faculty of Wayne State College (Nebraska) and Shepherd University (West Virginia).

Originally a bass trombonist, Dr. Gazda doubles on tenor trombone, euphonium, and tuba in solo, chamber, and large ensemble settings. He has performed with, among others, the Kennedy Center Opera House Orchestra, the Delaware Symphony, the Sioux City (Iowa) Symphony and Brass Quintet, the Maryland Symphony Orchestra and Brass Quintet, the Richmond (Virginia) Symphony, the Harrisburg (Pennsylvania) Symphony, and the Washington Bach Sinfonia. He has also performed with the Mormon Tabernacle Choir, the Jimmy Dorsey Orchestra, the Washington Trombone Ensemble, and The Supremes.

Dr. Gazda was a finalist in the Eastern Trombone Workshop National Solo Competition and the International Women's Brass Conference National Solo Competition. He has been a clinician at the New Jersey Music Educators Conference, the Delaware Music Educators Conference, the Nebraska Bandmasters Association Conference, and at many schools and events nationally. Dr. Gazda reviews both recordings and literature for the *International Trombone Association Journal* and has contributed to several other publications as a guest author or reviewer.

Dr. Gazda received his Bachelor's degree in music education from Shenandoah Conservatory, his Master of Music degree from the Manhattan School of Music, and his Doctorate in trombone performance and literature from the University of Maryland. His teachers have included David Summers, Stephen Norrell, and Matthew Guilford. He has pursued additional studies with David Fedderly, Michael Bunn, and Doug Elliott, and studied pedagogy and literature with Dr. Milton Stevens.

Dr. Alexander Lapins teaches at Northern Arizona University, Blue Lake Fine Arts Camp, Miraphone Academy of the West, and is tubist of the Elden Brass Quintet. A diverse artist, Dr.

Lapins is an enthusiast of early music, has taught a class in the history of rock music, and is the only tubist to have won fellowships at both the Tanglewood Music Center and the Henry Mancini Institute. He has performed with the Indianapolis Symphony Orchestra, Chicago Symphony Orchestra, Cincinnati Symphony Orchestra, Cincinnati Opera Orchestra, Disney Collegiate All-Star Band, the Guy Lombardo Orchestra, the New Sousa Band, and Harvey Phillips' Tubacompany. As a session musician, Dr. Lapins can  be heard on hundreds of recordings. Originally from the Virginian suburbs just outside Washington, D.C., he has performed in Europe, South America, China, and throughout the United States. He earned degrees from James Madison University, the University of Michigan, and Indiana University. Alexander Lapins is a Miraphone Artist.

 **Dr. J. Mark Thompson** joined the Northwestern State University (Natchitoches, Louisiana) faculty in fall 2000 and currently serves as Professor of Music. He teaches applied trombone, bass trombone, and tuba, along with related courses such as performance literature, pedagogy, recitals, and trombone choir. In addition, he serves the School of Creative and Performing Arts as Coordinator of Statistics and Acquisitions. In a career spanning two decades, he has taught at Coe College and Kirkwood Community College (both in Cedar Rapids, Iowa), and at Stephen F. Austin State University in Nacogdoches, Texas. He became a Nationally Certified Teacher of Music with a College Faculty Certificate in Brass awarded by the Music Teachers National Association in 1997, and in 2012 he was recognized with the awarding of the Permanent Professional Certificate. In April 2011, Dr. Thompson was honored as the first recipient of the Dr. Jean D'Amato Thomas Lifetime Achievement Award at Northwestern State University "in recognition of a career of outstanding scholarship and exceptional professional contributions." A charter life member of the International Trombone Association, Dr. Thompson chairs its Advisory Council on Literature, and has served on

its board of advisors. Editor and co-author of *French Music for Low Brass Instruments*, he also produced *Solos for the Student Trombonist,* second edition.

Dr. Thompson holds a Bachelor of Music, summa cum laude, from Murray State University, an M.S. in Systems Management from the University of Southern California, and M.A., M.F.A. and D.M.A. degrees from the University of Iowa. Formerly principal bass trombone of the Civic Orchestra of Chicago, he performs with the Shreveport Symphony (Louisiana), South Arkansas Symphony, Lancaster Festival (Ohio), and Des Moines Metro Opera Orchestras (Iowa).